Postmarked Home:

New & Selected Poems, 1979-2019

Poems by Michael Hathaway

Kansas City Spartan Press Missouri

Spartan Press
Kansas City, MO
spartanpresskc@gmail.com

Copyright © Michael Hathaway, 2019
First Edition 1 3 5 7 9 10 8 6 4 2
ISBN: 978-1-950380-08-4
LCCN: 2019935721

Design, edits and layout: Jason Ryberg
Cover artwork copyright © 2019: Olga Suvorova
https://academart.com/suvorova.html
Title page image: Marilyn Appelhans
Author photo: Shon Fox
All rights reserved. No part of this publication may be reproduced or transmitted in any form or by any means, electronic or mechanical, including photocopying, recording or by info retrieval system, without prior written permission from the author.

Special thanks to Jason Ryberg, Craig Ashby, Bryan Borland, and Cousin Anthony for their help and longsuffering patience. Most of these poems and stories first appeared in unrevised versions in other chapbooks and these journals and anthologies: *Alchemist Review; All Around the Editor's Desk; Always the Beautiful Answer: A Prose Poem Primer* (Kings Estate Press); *Anemone; Art:Mag; Arroyo's Violent Virgin Series; Aquarius Anthology; Artlife: The Original Limited Edition Monthly; Assaracus: A Journal of Gay Poetry; Atom Mind; Avalanche; Baker's Dozen* (Mulberry Press); *Beggars & Cheeseburgers; Between the Cracks: The Daedalus Anthology of Kinky Verse* (Daedalus Publ. Co.); *Blank Gun Silencer; Blind Horse Review; Calliope's Corner; Camellia; Chakra; Chance Magazine; Chiron Review, Cokefishing in Alpha Beat Soup; Contrarywise: An Anthology* (Kings Estate Press); *Daring Poetry Quarterly; A Day for a Lay: A Century of Gay Poetry* (Barricade Books); *Downtown Magazine; Expressions: first state journal; Famous Last Words; 5AM; Friendly Creatures* (Kings Estate Press); *fuel.; Gargoyle; gestalten [experimental poetry]* (Broken Boulder Press); *Gypsy; Haight-Ashbury Literary Journal; The Higginsville Reader; Home Planet News; Howling Dog; Impetus; Inglis House Poetry Workshop* (on-line); *The James White Review; Last Post Report; Lucid Moon; Lunatic Chameleon; Minotaur/Baker Street Irregular; misnomer; Mojave River Review* (on-line); *Mulberry Press Postcard Series; Mutated Viruses; Nerve Cowboy; New Sins; Non-prophet Postcard Series* (Broken Boulder Press); *Now and Then*; one (dog) press; *100 suns; One Tree Press Postcard Series; One Trick Pony; ONTHEBUS; Parnassus Literary Journal; Pearl; Pet Gazette; Piddiddle; Pink Pages (Beet); Plain Brown Wrapper; The Plowman* (Canada); *Poet; Potpourri; The Poet's Perspective: A Literary Capsule; Potpourri; Prairie Connection; Prairie Ink; Psychopoetica* (England); *Pudding; Quercus Review; RFD: A Country Journal for Gay Men Everywhere; Radio Void; Ransom; Re)Verb; Silver Wings; Simple Vows; Skidrow Penthouse; Skin &Bones; Spoon River Poetry Review; Staplegun; Stepping Stones; The Temple; Thirteen; Today's Prairie Woman/Prairie Woman; 22-5; Unexpected Harvest: A Gathering of Small Blessings* (Kings Estate Press); *Up Against the Wall, Mother; Van Gogh's Ear; A Voice; Voices: New Poems of Life & Experience; Vowel Movement* (Aileron Press); *Waterways: Poetry in the Mainstream; The Wire; Wheels* (Germany); *Wordgathering* (on-line); *Wormfeast;* and *Zen Tattoo.* The phrase, "Postmarked Home," paraphrased from the poem title "Letter from Buddy, Postmarked Heaven," *Still Life with Buddy: A Novel Told in Fifty Poems*, by Lesléa Newman (Orchard House Press, 1997), with permission of the author.

CONTENTS

Adam Had 'Em / 1

Letter to Anita Bryant / 2

Another Brick in the Wall / 4

At the End of the Day / 5

Balance in the Bible Belt / 6

The Ballad of Gypsy Rose / 7

Basher / 11

beast / 15

beyond sunday school / 16

Birthright / 17

Born Again / 18

a boy & some bullies / 20

The Burning Bed / 21

Carlotta's Revenge / 22

celebrating 47 years of friendship / 24

Cheap Therapy Cleverly Disguised as Prose Poem / 25

cinnamon man / 27

the club / 28

Cognitive Dissonance, or probably why people love coffee / 29

Cooking Secrets / 30

Letter to Dad / 33

Deconstructing the Patriarchy / 36

Election 1984 / 37

Election 2012 / 38

Elephant Joke / 39

Elusive Pisces / 40

Epitaph / 42

About Equality / 43

Everett / 44

excerpt / 45

All the Feminists in California & Me / 46

1st LUV/2boys / 47

First Spring / 48

Flaming Orgasm / 50

Fore! / 51

Friends in High Places / 52

Your Forrest Gump / 53

From the Mouths of Babes / 55

FUCK POETRY! / 57

The Gift / 58

God as Lover / 59

untitled: God loves little / 60

Gross / 61

haiku-esque / 62

Hands / 63

he holds me in such a way that shoves back
   the black hole of night / 64

About Heaven / 65

How It Happens / 67

A Hug on Williams Street / 69

i wish i'd met Antler when i was 13 / 71

i'm not a punching bag but … / 72

It's Been Said Peace Begins In Your Own Back Yard / 73

Judgment Day / 75

Kerouac's Gotta be Hiding Around Here Somewhere! / 76
Last Supper / 79
Leapfrog / 81
Letting Go / 84
Lions 1, Christians 0 / 86
Love Light / 87
me & Rhonda on astronomy & humanitarianism / 88
Melba's Cocktail / 89
message / 90
moon babies / 91
Letter to Mother, 7 Years Later, Postmarked Home / 92
My New Career / 101
The Mad Housesitter Has a Good Day / 102
me & ratboy run the gamut of literary lovers / 103
Medicare for All / 105
Midwesterner's Prune Face (MPF) / 106
You Know You're Loved When People Are Willing
   to Give You the Moon / 108
moon-in-aquarius / 110
moonlight dance / 112
night problem / 113
The Non-Smoker's Right / 114
note to a sleeping guy / 115
Ode to Grandpa Hathaway / 116
One of Cassandra's, er, I mean Mother's Dire Prophecies
   Actually Comes True / 117
Once When I was Samson / 119
The Perfect Tape / 120

poem scribbled on burger king napkin at 6:30 a.m. / 122
Poetry as Talisman / 123
postcard from California to my lover / 124
Proposed Legislation: Never to Forget / 125
The Pure Poetry That is Ratboy / 126
Revelations & Anticipation / 127
Road Trip: Topeka, November 29, 1997 / 128
St. John Pastoral / 130
Second to Last Poem for Tracy / 131
snapshot of me proofreading Chiron #53 ... / 132
stumbling into light / 134
summer 1986 / 135
Sunday School / 136
Talking to Squirrels / 137
They Don't Write Love Stories Like This Anymore / 139
Throwing Dirt: Remembering Julie / 140
To John – Just a Cat / 149
A Toast / 150
Tracy Pops Into a Dream Two Years Later
   Just to Let Me Know / 152
violent virgin / 154
Wanda / 155
What She Never Told Anyone / 156
what would Grandma think? / 158
When The Hunk Flunked Bar Exams Second Time / 160
Why I Love to Say Her Name Out Loud / 161
Winter Snapshot 2011 / 162

Introduction

The poet was full of apologies, as if asking me to write an introduction to the book in your hands was a chore and not an honor. There are certain people who broke down walls – no – who reduced entire structures to rubble so that I could emerge years later as a gay man in Not-A-Big-City, America, writing poetry, publishing work that makes me feel electric, reading next to my poet-husband, and letting the neighbor's cat, Audrey, inside on rainy or cold or pleasant nights to sleep on my folded jeans in our closet. Michael Hathaway, the poet, the writer, the editor and publisher, is one such person, and thus he falls into that elite category of *ask for the clothes off my back and receive them*.

It isn't a chore for me to tell you how Michael's poems found me, as art supernaturally finds the people it rescues and not the other way around, through Gavin Dillard's anthology, *A Day for a Lay: A Century of Gay Poetry* [Barricade Books 1998]. I don't remember how the book came into my possession. It could have been one of the dozens or so I stole from the rural library near my home, too fearful to approach the librarian, a friend of my mother, with any book containing a variation or synonym of the word homosexual in its title. It might have been ordered from some contraband corner of the World Wide Web in the wild, wild west days of the Internet, because that's another place I found my lifelines. Either way, a lifeline it was, and I found myself with my bedroom door locked and my light on late into the night, devouring poems by the likes of Allen Ginsberg and Thom Gunn and Reginald Shepherd. And Michael Hathaway.

Everyone, every single writer in that book was a giant to me. Until then, I'd read what I could of gay poets in piecemeal fashion, poem by poem, but there had been no definitive Bible of Gay Verse. Reading the anthology presented me with a kind of queer Olympus, and these were the poets who'd made it there.

To be published in a book like *A Day for a Lay* and end up in the public library of Small Town, Southern State, where a kid like me could find it, that was the definition of success. These writers were immortal and were my instant heroes. If we are lucky, as I have been, our early heroes remain our lifelong heroes. Sometimes our heroes even become our friends.

The first poem of Michael's I read was "me & ratboy run the gamut of literary lovers," which, of course, introduced me to Ratboy, this magnetic, crude, mostly straight, cocky, and very sexual creature, a walking, talking version of Freud's Id. Ratboy shows up in four of Michael's five poems in *A Day for a Lay*, drinking, punching, hitting the road, moving *as if our lives depend on it*, chasing something new and magical, something wild and untamable. I had a Ratboy, too. Didn't we all? Don't we all think of someone when we read the lines, *[I] beg him to let me / help every inch / of his long brown body into heaven* or *[i] take his touch, his skin / any way he offers it*? My Ratboy's name was Ricky. Ricky's in prison right now for the third or fourth time, and though I denied it when he asked me if I wrote about him in any of my books, the truth is he's all over my first book. Where did I learn to write about Ricky? From Ratboy. Come to think of it, where did I learn to write about the little town where I grew up and out-stayed my welcome? From Michael.

Michael has this way of creating something special out of the ordinary. It's the same thing Springsteen does when he writes about factory work or the deathtrap of his hometown. Michael paints a similar picture of his hometown, with its extended families and happy-sad eulogies and monotonous breakrooms and Kansas dirt and neighbors who voluntarily escape or flee out of dark necessity, but if Springsteen's Jersey is a deathtrap, Michael's Kansas is a lifetrap.

Michael's work holds nights that sweat stars and exhale hungry fantasies of people from other places, be they JFK Jr. or the poet Antler, who, by the way, I also wish I'd met when I was 13, and who else is brave enough to open the door for me to say this? Art should make you gasp sometimes in the discomfort of recognition. Michael's work does this, like a slug to the shoulder or a jolt somewhere below the belt.

If Michael's poems in *A Day for a Lay* told me a great deal about the poet, a line in his biographical note from the same book told me just as much, the part that revealed he lived in the midwest with his twelve cats. He is the poet who, when his aunt dies, says matter-of-factly, *She left eight cats, so now I have eight more cats.* The poet who chases his fat, fluffy Charlie to (successfully) save a baby squirrel. The poet who makes me gag with "Gross" (you'll just have to read it). The poet who makes me cry, damn him, with "To John – Just a Cat" (you'll just have to read that one, too, but get a tissue).

Michael became somewhat infamous with his cat poems. Once, when I was at a literary event in New York and was talking to a group of gay poets about our mutual influences, when I mentioned Michael, one of them said, lovingly, *Oh, you mean the Cat Poet?* Yes, the Cat Poet. There is a certain literary magazine of prominence in the United States that until recently included a warning within their submission guidelines to not submit poems about cats. I have a feeling they've been deprived of Michael's take on felines, or perhaps they've read his work and simply know that no one can do it better.

It's fitting, then, that I'm writing this introduction the day after our household said goodbye to The Lady Chablis, a gray, asthmatic kitty whose lifelong struggle for breath aged her body too quickly. I'd inherited her from my father, who gave me cash to begin Sibling Rivalry Press ten days before he, himself, unexpectedly died. In many ways she was not the mascot of the press but the heart of it, a link to my father and the loving gift he gave me that, in circular fashion, led me to some degree of poetry-notoriety that in turn allowed me to establish a relationship with many of my early heroes, including Michael.

Of all the potential writers and projects it was the Cat Poet and this project I serendipitously had on my schedule for today, the day after The Day Lady died. Now and forever there will be another memory associated with the work of Michael Hathaway in the same manner we all attach our own meaning and memory to work which moves us.

I'll read his poems and I'll think of our Lady, as you'll read his work and think of someone you love or have loved, be it the beast you spoil who keeps your feet warm or the phantom weight of them, years gone now. Or of your best friend, the one with whom fate saddled you, the one you told your every scandalous secret. Or of your own Ratboy, who when you finally kissed him tasted like everything you were told you weren't supposed to have. But, oh. You had him. We had them, and we carry them with us, all of them. This is the great revelation of Michael Hathaway's work: We had them, we loved them, and we don't regret a thing.

Bryan Borland,
Publisher,
Sibling Rivalry Press

*for the four little suns,
Kristi, Seth, Lucas, & Alyssa*

Adam Had 'Em

The naming of the beasts is exhausting.
After 80+ cats in 20 years,
I am running out of names.

Christmas Eve, 2000,
I took in three unnamed female cats
disguised as *baby-sitting* for a friend.
When I realized it was permanent,
at first it seemed I might have to
resort to Fluffy and Snowball and Precious ...

But fate stepped in
the day I decided to administer
de-worming pills.

As I stood there exhausted,
bleeding and utterly defeated,
their names came down
like 40 whacks:

Lizzie
Lucrezia
& Lilith

Letter to Anita Bryant

This has been 20 years in the making. I was 15 through most of 1977, a Baptist by choice. Gay by birth. Not happy gay, just gay. I was smart, friendly, out-going and talented. I wrote poems, played piano, spun records for hours on end, loved my cat Pandora to distraction, adored and respected my parents, enjoyed my friends.

Being alive was a gift. I knew that even at 15. All I wanted was for every creature that drew breath to be happy and never suffer. (I was no angel, but a Virgo/Libra child is the next best thing.)

Your face began appearing in the paper, on the news, screaming an unholy rage. I was a child and didn't understand how you could hate someone you never met.

I didn't hate you. I liked your song "Paper Roses." It was one of the records I played. I thought it was honest and cute how you stamped your little foot when you didn't win the Miss America pageant that one year.

I was 15 and didn't even know what bigotry was until you taught me. Your Christian face blowing hatred out of our tv what seemed like every night. Teaching self-hatred to children. It inspired me to dig beneath the surface of Christianity, then logically abandon it.

At 36, I understand a little because I caught myself hating back at your brick wall, slammed door face. It doesn't feel good though. I'm handing that dubious Christian gift back to you. I don't want it. I don't hate you, and I won't hate anyone. You can't make me.

My good parents taught two wrongs don't make a right. My hating you back won't erase the pain of inequality and discrimination.

Twenty years later, Anita Bryant, I can say this: I'm happy gay now. Being gay is my birthright. Being alive never felt better. And I love you— you paper roses, amazing grace, foot-stomping beauty queen you.

Another Brick in the Wall

She instructed her English class to write a weekly magazine article report from a periodical of choice. One week I forgot about the report, which was due in 5th hour English, right after lunch. at lunch, I grabbed the only magazine available at home at the moment and wrote a report about *All in the Family* – how Norman Lear was a genius, revolutionizing American television, daring to deal with the controversial; using television to create social change; and most astonishing of all, how he battled bigotry by creating a lovable bigot in Archie Bunker as a mirror for much of the U.S. I received a *zero* on the entire report specifically for choosing *TV Guide* as my magazine of *choice,* and not *Time* or *Newsweek*. I wish I could go back 20 years and tell Mrs. McCandless, *Bitch! I'll take an A+ on this report, thank you very much — foremost, for a well-written report on an intelligent subject which is also a U.S. institution; second, for creativity and improvisation in the face of disaster; and third, for giving a shit at all.* Or maybe I'd just write a report from *Hustler* that would singe her face off.

At the End of the Day

All that really matters is
the dishes are washed,
the floors are swept
and all the chores are done.

All that really matters is
that every little soul in your care
is fed, tuckered out
from the day's big fun
and sleeps peacefully
in the television's soft blue glow.

Balance in the Bible Belt

Annabelle,
New York Jewish lady,
transplanted to central Kansas
sits in the flea market
amidst her leather & bead creations, rolls her eyes,
says, *Oy! I read the Satanic Bible*
during the Christmas season,
just to maintain
*some **balance!***

The Ballad of Gypsy Rose
in memory of Connie Star (1948-2017)

On Sunday, July 2, around 9 a.m. my friend Connie Star took a swan dive into that Great Chocolate Fountain in the Sky. She's probably doing the backstroke even as we speak. I'm tempted to tell the story of her life, which is fascinating, and which she always wanted me to do. But that would be a bit overwhelming so soon after her passing, so instead, I'll tell the story of how we met and share a glimpse into the person she was.

In February, 1984, I was 22 years old, worked during the day as a typesetter at the daily newspaper and inhabited a trailer house on Maple Street in Great Bend, Kansas. (I'd also been publishing *The Kindred Spirit*, which would morph into *Chiron Review*, for two years.) I had a house full of roommates who wouldn't work or help with any expenses. They ran up the phone bill, let my cats out, magically appeared on my payday, then magically disappeared when the money was gone a few days later.

On February 4, at 3 a.m., one of my roommates woke me to say, *My friend Connie's on the phone, she wants to meet you. It's collect ...* I grumbled, stumbled to the phone and mumbled, *Hello?* The voice on the other end said, *Hi! I'm Gypsy Rose! Patty says you write poetry! I write poetry too! Listen!* She recited a poem she had written.

Then she said, *I sing too! Some people say I sound just like Janis Joplin, listen!* She sang every verse of, "I Gave My Love a Cherry (The Riddle Song)." It was one of those rare magical moments in life when time seems to stand still. I was utterly mesmerized by her voice. She had a deep, robust, intense alto voice that set off sparks, very much like Janis Joplin's did, the kind of bluesy, whiskey-laced voice you hear in smoke-filled barrooms. We talked and talked and talked until the alarm clock rang for me to get ready for work at 7 a.m. She promised to come visit, but I didn't expect to ever meet her.

Three days after that phone call, a knock came at my front door. There she stood, all 250 animated pounds of her. She had long, flowing, bright red hair adorned with colorful roach-clip feathers, light green cat eyes that saw directly into your soul, and a brown suede jacket with the fringe just swinging! She wore multiple necklaces, bracelets, long dangling earrings and a ring on every finger. She sparkled and jangled and said, *Hi! I'm Gypsy Rose!* She burst in, made herself at home, and dumped the entire contents of her oversized hippie fringe suede bag on my kitchen table. That's when the stories started. That's how the friendship of a lifetime was born.

She moved in with us, but my other friends were so jealous and so mean to her she moved right back out after three days. She didn't stay long enough to pay rent, but gave me her Beatles *White Album* in exchange for staying there and a few phone calls. I tried to refuse it, but she insisted.

A couple weeks later, I saw her in the grocery store. We chatted a bit. Even though she was homeless and had become an expert at surviving and living by her wits, she never told a lie or stole a single thing in her life. She knew I was having serious troubles with my *friends*. She pulled the food stamps from her wallet and counted them out.

She gave me half of them, which I think was about $8 worth. Again, I tried to refuse, but she insisted. That's when I knew for sure she was a keeper.

She's the first person I came out to. It was a matter of self-defense, she was determined to marry me. I worried about losing her friendship, but coming out to her made our bond even stronger. She said I spoiled other men for her. She called me her *honorary husband*. We celebrated our anniversaries on most Valentine's days and sent each other *husband* and *wife* Valentine cards. She declared a few years ago we were the hillbilly version of *Will & Grace*. I liked that.

We were best buddies for 33 years. We both loved being where the people and the parties were, but neither one of us were ever interested in recreational drugs. We did a little drinking early on, but got bored with it. We didn't care what anyone else might indulge in as long as we could be at the party. And of course, it wasn't all smooth sailing. Neither one of us knew what a *boundary* was. We could argue and fight like cats. But even in the throes of our worst caterwauling, we both knew our friendship was forever, no matter what.

In her next incarnation, I'm thinking she'll be the benevolent and beloved queen of a small country. She had a serious *queen complex* and practiced for it all this lifetime. Wherever she lived was always a gathering place, where she held court and counseled anyone who needed counseling. She was awake and available late into the wee small hours of the night, and prevented more than one suicide in her life.

I really hate to see her go. I find myself still checking my phone first thing in the morning for text messages from her. Sadness is inevitable, but so is gratitude. An epic friendship like this is one of life's greatest gifts. I'm ever so grateful to the Powers That Be that we met and were able to live out such an incredibly long and loyal friendship, to experience such powerful love.

Basher

We were two ships who passed catastrophically in the night. I'd heard about him and the gay men he and his friends beat and robbed at the park. I wished to myself, *I sure would like to meet that bastard.*

At 4 a.m. one morning, I did. I was sitting there alone, enjoying the solitude and peacefulness of the July night at the park when he and his band of bullies came screeching in like maniacs. They pulled up beside my car and he sneered, *You're a fag.* I sneered, *You're right.*

I was afraid, but more angry when I realized who he was: the cruel gay basher, the one who beat and robbed my retarded friend, the one who beat, robbed and pissed on another gentle friend of mine. I wanted to hurt him any way I could and the only way I could was with words.

But still I loved him the second I looked into his eyes, even though they gleamed dangerously with psychotic hostility and he spewed condemnation and religious diatribe and every word of hate he could conjure up.

We were like two foghorns blasting our viewpoints into each others' stone faces.

This went on for about an hour as he insisted he was doing God's work, *cleaning up the world, punishing fags.* That was his crusade, and I was blaring that his God was not everyone's God, that his God was probably dead anyway, and that his Bible, to many, was so much drivel.

And, never flinching, I insisted that he was more offensive to a just god, more guilty of wrongdoing, more hell-bent than I, using his warped sense of religion to justify his need to hurt people.

I said calmly, *You're too violent. It's wrong to hurt people, you know. You'll outgrow it. I think you'll change.*

He spat, *I will not! I like violence!* His eyes gleamed, mocking me.

I laughed. His bluntness amused me.

Though I never left my car and kept the doors locked and windows most of the way up, at first I felt like it was inevitable that he would hurt me. So I got reckless, more antagonistic. I said, *I'll bet a frustrated fag yourself. Psychologists say that the more violently opposed a man is to gays, the more likely it is that he is gay himself.* I didn't know if that was true, but it sounded good and I enjoyed saying it to him.

He said, *I am not! They're liars! You know what I do to fags? I beat them, take their money and piss on them!*

I countered with, *Pissing on someone is considered a sexual act. So, technically, you're had sexual experiences with other men. Technically, you're a fag.*

He yelled, *That does it!* and scrambled out of his truck to attack me. I put my car in drive and hit the gas. The merry chase was on.

I drove 30 miles per hour the two miles into town so they couldn't run me off the road. I thought about driving to the police station for I knew there was no other way I would be able to shake the relentless bashers. But I wasn't through with them yet, so I drove to the library parking lot where they once again pulled up to my car. Clearly annoyed, he said tersely, *You drove 30 miles per hour all the way to town.* I smiled, *I know.*

He said, *That really pisses me off.*

I said, *Good! Then my mission is accomplished.*

He said, *Hey! Are you rich? Do you have any money?*

I like to take people's money. I'd beat the shit out of you even for a dollar ...

I said, *I'd give you a dollar just to get you to shut up.*

But the conversation changed its angry tone. It softened after he said, *if I had a son and he was a fag, I'd kill him.*

I said, *if you couldn't love a son after you found out he was gay, then you would have never loved him in the first place. Haven't you ever heard of unconditional love?*

He said, *I'd love him, but I'd still kill him.* He gave me a sheepish smile.

I laughed and knew then he was lying. He smiled a human smile and laughed too. He became more friendly, less abusive.

We exchanged first names, which were the same. He said, *I like you. You're gay, not a fag. If I see you again, I promise not to beat you up.*

I said, *Thanks. I'd appreciate it if you'd leave my friends alone, too.*

He asked, *Which ones are your friends?*

I said, *All of them*, as we parted company.

* * * * * *

Yesterday was a dull day. It had been a year or more since my life clashed with Mike's that July night in 1990. His face and flashing black eyes had been haunting my thoughts and I felt something of an obsession just to talk with him again.

I went out to the Roadrunner Café after midnight and ordered French fries and cottage cheese. I sat there talking with a friend and was surprised to see Mike behind the counter, cooking. We looked at each other and I wasn't sure it was him, since his eyes were kinder, his face softer, the psychotic edge gone.

I didn't have the nerve to talk to him, but finally, he boldly walked to my table and asked what my name was. I told him.

He stood there in his little white apron and said, *I'm not a homophobe anymore*, and grinned and flicked his wrist as I remembered how I had spat that word at him.

He said, *Man, I'm not like that anymore. I don't see anything wrong with it. I'm really sorry for all that shit, man. I don't do it anymore. You're the last one I did it to. Really. I gave you extra fries. See?*

He stood there, his eyes deep, big, round, and pleading. And as my heart jumped out of my throat and landed at his feet, I said, *That's okay, man. It really is okay.*

beast

    pirate-eyed
    July moon cat

    funny clown
    & star lover

    wise secret
    nightkeeper

    tender chin
    kisser

    protective
    nightwatcher

    pillow hogger

    perfect
    life companion

beyond sunday school

He seems like a scary giant
who can create Life and Death out of boredom,
invent Love when he's lonely,
Hate because he's angry

Then he seems like a primitive child,
playing about with his planets/marbles,
exploding gasses, pretty colors and sounds.

Throughout his playground universe,
space stuff pops, flies, explodes, crashes
to his amused delight.

Light years away from the scope
of any human eye or comprehension,
creation burns, freezes,
creates color & light,
changes,
remains the same.

Huge orbs travel given paths,
minute by minute,
eon by eon,

as little bugs live and die
as we live and die
God plays.

Birthright

My horoscope declares,
Your father will be able to
leave you very little.

When my father remarried and moved across town,
he gave me a little house on two acres,
the house I grew up in,
the safest place on earth,
where Mother's ashes are planted
and the remains of every pet
I ever loved.

Along with an armful of Hank Williams, Sr.
and Connie Smith records,
this came with a lifetime of lessons by example
in integrity, a work ethic beyond reproach,
and an undeniable sense that I was loved
no matter what.

Born Again

My karma ran over my dogma
        – bumper sticker

During the last couple years
I lost the few stubborn remnants
of midwest baptist dogma.

I've become a belligerent,
slap-happy anti-religionist,
with way too much logic and science
at my disposal.

June 3, 1999 is a peace-filled
sunny day in central Kansas.
There are faint noises in the backyard,
the mewing of newborn kittens.

Naomi and year-old daughter Wynonna
both have babies, about two weeks old.
Both families live among the ruins
of a collapsed shed, overgrown with weeds –

five new noisy cosmic children
meeting creation,
wide-eyed, hungry,
climbing at the sun.

I kneel to be near them,
awash in beatific awe.

Maybe I'm not such a heathen after all?
I'm at church, on my knees, moved to tears –
god was born in my backyard.

a boy & some bullies

He goes for an evening walk
to be with wind and stars and moon.
The bullies don't approve
of how he walks or
how his long hair
dances with the wind.
They drive by mocking,
taunting, yelling,
FAGGOTMOTHERFUCKER!
The boy ignores them,
keeps walking.
The bullies drive on
deeper into their darkness.

The Burning Bed
for Connie Star

It's not just a book
on her shelf.
One hardly notices it
visiting with her
in her living room.

After half a lifetime
of being beat on
by parents, brothers,
husbands & lovers,
of being a martyr to
their frustrations & failures,

The Burning Bed is not
just a book
on her shelf,

it's a promise ...

Carlotta's Revenge

Rusty and I felt like we'd *come home*
during our 1991 road trip to San Francisco.
We were delighted to be in *Queer Central*,
surrounded by *family*,
feeling as if we were a *majority*
for once in our lives.

We were like children there. He splashed
and frolicked in the ocean for the first time;
I scoured every bookstore for small press
and poetic treasures.

Our last day there we were not happy
about leaving and consoled ourselves
in the Atherton Hotel bar –
I with Margarita and he with Carlotta's Revenge.
Closing time found me trying to convince him
we should go up to our room. He refused,
wanting to finish Carlotta, the sixth.

The bartender said we could take Carlotta with us,
so I took the drink and led Rusty donkey-with-carrot-style
to our sixth floor room.
He followed with a goofy smile, arms swimming,
grabbing at the drink.

He asked permission to throw the glass
out the window. I yelled, *No!* and lunged for it.
So he sat on the floor casually leaning out the
big window yelling at hookers on the corner below.
I pulled him away. He decided
he was hungry and began munching on a cold pizza.

Thinking it was safe, I left him alone
and went into the bathroom to get ready for bed.
When I came out, Rusty was giggling with joy,
tossing pizza slices out the window
at the open sunroof of a black limousine
parked on the street below.

celebrating 47 years of friendship

Deb never gets mad
when I break someone's rules.

When I say something that makes
teachers/preachers gasp
& start a file on me
she laughs & puffs on her
Winston

I can be w/her & remain
whole.

She falls a lot,
has been known to utter
the dreaded *f-word,*
but the laughter never leaves her eyes,
nor does the mellow earth brown
love of God.

Cheap Therapy Cleverly Disguised as Prose Poem

i bumble and stumble my way to enlightenment. i resent half-baked shit i was taught. and a few things i wasn't taught. that *Israel* means to *wrestle with God,* and questioning and wrestling with him is practically mandatory, since most of his best people did it. and how sometimes God backed off. i resent the Standard Backwoods Baptist Answer to Childish Questions: to question God is a *sin.* silly children assume an omnipotent deity should be logical and consistent, and should balance out in heart and mind.

    i sort of resent not being taught the Third Commandment in original Hebrew is *Thou shalt not carry the Lord's name in vain,* not *take* it in vain, as was translated into English by medieval dumbasses. that muttering *God damn it,* or *Jesus Jumped-Up Christ!* might not be quite the cosmic offense against God as luring a gentle funny loving gay man into the country, ganging up on him two-to-one, beating him with crowbar and bat, trashing his car, urinating on him, leaving him for dead, saying we are *doing God's work: exterminating faggots.* (i wonder just how many God damn Baptists it will take to figure that one out.)

    and call me crazy, but i resent not being taught in Sunday school that King James I, whose name graces the second English translation of the *Holy Bible,* was queer like me. and if God could trust his eternal word to a *faggot,* then maybe there's a place for me in the plan after all?

                                  i resent red-face preachers screaming about hellfire and damnation because of Adam and Eve's *original sin,* raging and pounding on their Bibles, scaring the holy shit out of the child i was. never noting Adam and Eve allegedly lived more than 900 happy years together; were Mother and Father of all humanity; and represent the concept that we are all – every religion, nationality, ability, size, shape, race, gender and sexual orientation – brothers and sisters, one big family. No one can change that – not even Nazis, Ku Klux Klan or Christians of any caliber.

                                                  i mostly resent being threatened as a child: i wonder why i was told i was dangling over a smelly pit of raging fire – that one tiny transgression would plunge me into that fire. i'd be wailing, gnashing my teeth and consumed by maggots for eternity – when i could have been taught the Bible in two simple words: forgiveness and love.

cinnamon man

the last time i saw tracy
it was spring & all six feet of him
was sprawled in a pear tree;
his brown cinnamon form
barely clothed in snug denim cutoffs.
he was smoking weed;
mutilating pear blossoms;
showering himself & me
with the shredded white remains.
from the ground i asked him
to climb down
so he could get a secret from me.
he howled like a moon-crazed werewolf;
said he was real busy
at the moment.
i knew that.
but it didn't stop my wanting him.
it didn't stop my needing
his wicked knock about love.
it didn't stop me from nibbling
the mangled blossoms
off his dangling cinnamon feet.

the club

when Ratboy ran off with the carnival it hit me hard.

i was inundated with heartbroken bimbos
ringing my doorbell: where is he?!?
when is he coming home?!?

the first one cried on my shoulder,
i tried to comfort her, said,
you know he is a wild spirit,
no one can hold him. that's partly why we love him,
why we have to let him go.
she said gently, *i know you miss him too.*
she left, tears glistening down her cheeks.

the second said sarcastically,
do you know where he is? he tells you everything ...
i said, *yes, i know where he is.*
he's flown head first into the future
embracing his destiny with a big fat bear hug.
there's nothing you, nor I,
nor anyone else can do to stop him.

the third was hysterical,
a brain-dead, bug-eyed girl,
where is he? where is he? oh gawd,
when is he coming home? i've been
crying for three days!!!
i sneered, *join the club, bitch!*
and slammed the door.

Cognitive Dissonance, or
probably why people love coffee

Some nights misery piles on misery,
decades of loss and grief,
cruel and chronic depression,
tectonic plates of existential angst.

A country bumpkin in Sam Brownback's rural Kansas,
has no business
even knowing what that is.

And then there was that little quest for wisdom —
it really opened up a can of worms —
I eagerly & naively popped the top right off The Void,
peeked into the nihilists' abyss.

It's too late to un-see it now.
I'm that Looney Tunes character
free-falling endlessly,
seated at a bistro table, legs crossed,
calmly enjoying a nice cup of tea,
reading a good book
while everything never stops falling.

But all is well.
Time and age teach
All this silly horror
dissipates with the morning sun,
chores, and hot black coffee.

Cooking Secrets

In spring 1999, my best friend met *Richard From Burbank* through an on-line lonely-hearts ad. Richard From Burbank invited him to California so they could meet in person. My friend was hesitant to go alone, so this potential new amour paid my way to accompany him.

Richard From Burbank turned out to be decent, fun and interesting with decent, fun and interesting friends, with names like Carol, Andrea and Mother Don, a big burly baritone bartender at Venture Inn.

On Saturday night, Andrea, offered to make everyone dinner at Richard's house. She was a large and lovely fiftysomething transvestite, most exquisitely dressed and made-up. She invited my friend and I to accompany her to the market in her neighborhood. In the car, she said, *It's not safe. You stay behind me!* So there was this plus-size drag queen in a short, tight, bright hot pink skirt and high heels with two Kansas country boys following meekly in-tow.

The moment we entered the store, she transitioned. Her dainty walk turned into a macho, bow-legged swagger. She puffed out her chest and swung her arms. We followed her single file through the store as she compared prices and shopped for dinner. We survived our sojourn into the *bad neighborhood,* and returned to Richard's house.

While the others talked, laughed, and drank cocktails on the patio, I stood at the kitchen island and listened to Andrea talk as she prepared the food. She laid out great slabs of beef steak, peppered both sides until they were black, then attacked them ferociously with a stainless steel meat hammer. She said, *This is the secret to good steak,* and eyes twinkling, *This is how you beat your meat!*

She pounded those steaks over and over and over. As she pounded, she talked. She said, *So you're a writer? Maybe you will write my story?*

She hadn't seen her parents since she was 16. They disowned her and threw her out of their house when she came out of the closet. Andrea was homeless in San Francisco until Janis Joplin and her blond lady lover took her into their apartment. Andrea said Janis was very sweet to her.

Andrea had an affair with an actor who starred in a popular musical sitcom in the early 1970s. He was so sweet and sexy and she was so in love, she lost herself in him. But the sitcom's producer didn't want a transvestite hanging around his teen heartthrob star. Andrea explained she was a threat to '70s sitcom *family values* – meaning studio profits. The producer threatened one way or another, she would *disappear*. Fearing for her life, she did disappear.

Her eyes filled with tears. She said she wished she'd known then that nothing they could have done to her would have been worse than disappearing without saying goodbye, without telling her boyfriend why she left.

The more she talked, the more the tears ran, the angrier she got, the harder she pounded those poor steaks.

Maybe her stories were true, maybe not, I don't know. What I do know is those were the most tender steaks in the history of cooking – and the pain in her eyes was real.

Letter to Dad
Father's Day – 2001

Some writer friends have speculated that because I don't talk or write about you, because we have little in common, because we don't spend a lot of time together, that we are not close, must not get along or have some unspeakably horrible history between us.

I want to set the record straight, so I'm writing about you now. I hope it doesn't embarrass you.

They should know, gathering from bits and pieces of barely spoken family history, that an ever-diminishing, generations-old cycle of emotional and/or physical abuse ended with you. There was never even a trace of it in you. Maybe mom helped, maybe it was all on your own. It doesn't matter. You had the heart and mind to break it. Too few children have the luxury of believing the world is a safe and loving place through childhood, but thanks to you and mom, that luxury was mine.

They didn't see you working two and three jobs to support your family your whole adult life. They didn't see you as a young father enthralled with his two sons, playing and wrestling and instilling a foundation of love, caring and affection that a 10-point earthquake could never shake.

They don't know the lengths you'd go to see your sons smile, to hear them laugh. After returning from a family outing to see *101 Dalmatians* in the early 1970s, they didn't see you donning a fake-fur coat, smoking a pencil and vamping around singing, *Cruella DeVille, Cruella DeVille* ... Years later they didn't hear you wailing along with my Janis Joplin records, sneering, *Sounds like she dropped something on her foot!*

They never saw you letting me play Janis or any records I wanted, as loud as I wanted or read any book I wanted as late as I wanted. They don't know you bought my first typewriter, paid for the publication of my first poetry book.

They never heard you impart timeless wisdom, *All that long hair will give you headaches!*

In spite of our disagreements and skirmishes, they don't know I've looked up to you as my ultimate hero, even into adulthood. They've never heard me say, *Well my dad says ...* as if this is the be-all, end-all source and there's no wisdom whatsoever in arguing with it.

I want them to know that even though I wasn't what you expected or wanted in a son — what father expects his son to be a gay, vegetarian, soft-hearted, strong-willed, radically liberal, loud-mouthed poet?!? — you rose to the occasion, handled it with more love and wisdom than most any other son of the American 1950s would have had the guts to. And even though I can't and won't be sorry for who I am, I can thank my lucky stars for my good fortune in the Parents Department.

And a couple months ago, on that drizzly April evening, I was digging a grave for my beautiful golden-white kitten who'd been hit by a car. I never felt more alone, wishing mom was alive again, thinking how I'd give anything and everything to talk to her for just a few minutes. I looked up from my sad thoughts and grim task to see a little red car, whirling a U-turn at 8th & Prairie. You stopped and chatted while I was digging. You said, *Is that the only shovel you got?* I said, *Yeah, it does okay.* You said, *I'll get you a better one.*

Someone might think this was a conversation about a shovel. But these words were not about a shovel. They spoke of a love that is beyond words. A love that does not need to be analyzed, belabored or shouted from the rooftops, but that just is.

Maybe mom sent you. Maybe instinct. It doesn't matter. The fact remains that you appeared, and as always, made everything all right again just by being there. This is the stuff perfect fathers are made of.

Deconstructing the Patriarchy

For Linda Bloodworth-Thomason

Why do men strut around like cocks of the walk —
their egos ever-spewing geysers —
when women are the makers of life
& men are mostly fertilizer?

Election 1984

My friend, the 92-year-old
million dollar woman
voted a straight-line
die-hard Republican ballot
and had since Harding.

It pleased me to know in 1984
my $0 Democrat vote
canceled every conservative
X she marked.

Election 2012

The Wackadoodles
(Latin: *wacus dudlei*)
are creeping out of the woodwork
and into our elections!

They are convinced
Jesus Is Coming Soon.
(If you don't believe me,
read their bumper stickers.)

If He's smart, He won't.

When He tells them to
STOP worshipping The Market,
STOP stealing
from the elderly, sick and disabled,
STOP stealing
from children, the poor & downtrodden,
STOP bullying women and gays,
STOP bullying immigrants and Muslims,
STOP bullying the working classes,

those paragons of virtue
will crucify Him all over again.

Elephant Joke

What do you call
two abusive trainers
being mauled and killed
beneath the trunk and feet
of a frantic, angry
elephant?

A good start.

Elusive Pisces

for Tracy

Despite upstream wishes for you,
I never know where you are.
About once a year I get a letter
from some jail or other raunchy place.
I guess you're just checking in,
you know how I worry.
I hate to see you drifting further and further downstream.
Your wicked smile is my favorite thing about you,
but every year your face gets a little harder,
your hazel eyes a little duller.
I thought I had forgotten you,
finally set you free to lazily drift downstream
into oblivion. But last night I lay in bed
longing to know your address;
wondering if you sleep nude
on these breathless June nights.
I got up, walked outside, arms raised to Venus
and whispered, *Bring elusive Pisces home.*
I clung to stars, searched for secrets,
begged and pleaded,
then returned to my empty bed. Someday elusive Pisces,
I'll find a place where three rivers meet,
with a wind that I can scream into for days.

I'll raise my hands to Venus and chant that spell,
scream your name until I lose my voice,
scream your name into the winds
where three rivers meet,
'til God cracks a smile or gets annoyed,
I won't sleep or eat but scream your name
until someone tells me you'll be mine.

Epitaph

For God's sake
don't inscribe this on my tombstone,
Rest in Peace or *Be with Jesus*.

Inscribe this: *He learned to love
in spite of Christians, Republicans
and rednecks.*

Inscribe: *He knew how it felt
to trip over his stupid heart,
to fall flat on his face,
to lie in quiet contentment all night
beside the man he loved.*

Inscribe: *He learned to feel joy without shame.*

About Equality

Since mystery creates fear,
fear creates hatred,
and hatred creates violence,
let's take the mystery out of it.

Gay sex is
no more or less disgusting,
no more or less shocking,
no more or less offensive,
no more or less messy,
no more or less interesting
than what Mike Pence
or Ted Cruz
do to their wives
in the missionary position.

Ok. It may be a bit more *interesting*.

Everett

Everett was drunk, sprawled on my couch at 2 a.m.
I didn't know Everett well enough
for him to be sprawled drunk on my couch at 2 a.m.,
but my friend Debra found him at the bar next door
waving a big knife around,
trying to fight with some cops,
so she led him away from a parole violation
to my house.

He couldn't stand up and collapsed on the couch
as he recited poetry he'd written years ago.

Then he said, *You should be a dealer, man!*
I could triple and quadruple your investment,
if you know what I mean (wink wink),
I'm going to Houston for a shipment –
your house is in the perfect location ...
He pointed to his eyes and said,
Listen to me, man ...

My old gray cat Cecil jumped onto Everett's leg,
walked the length of his lanky body,
stood staring at him eyeball to eyeball.
Then he began licking Everett's earlobe.

Overcome with emotion, Everett whimpered,
This cat likes me! I'm a lower life form
and this cat likes me!

excerpt

eventually i take a mighty poetic leap
into midnight dreams
singing loudly at the moon's face
grabbing tiny stars & planets
i put them in a jar
poke holes in the lid
watch them glow like fireflies
in their orbits

All the Feminists in California & Me

She hated a poem I published
in *Chiron Review*
which she claimed
condoned violence to women
and threatened
if I ever came to California,
she and all the feminists
in California
would rip my throat out.

1ST LUV/2 boys

We traded secrets and jokes
laughed afternoon into evening.
You held my hand,
let me touch the pounding
of your big sweet heart.
We laid close together in dirt.
Nothing mattered
but your mouth on mine,
my hands on your hot back.
We let midnight drip from stars
over that field
of sleeping black-eyed susans.

First Spring

He was brilliant fire-orange and snow white, a roly-poly kitten named after singer Fatboy Slim —more Fatboy than Slim when he was abandoned in my yard in late July, 2000.

Too wild to be friends at first, it took two months and the onset of the second worst winter since 1919 to convince him we could be best buds. After our initial touch, he transformed into an undulating bag of charm and affection, his purring reverberating throughout the house. It was as if we'd always been devoted friends, as if he'd never mistrusted me.

He became my constant companion, under my feet, on my lap, on my pillow, when he wasn't busy being a kitten. He loved the other cats too, eagerly adopted his new brothers and sisters, especially young Lulu, Joni, his laid-back, long-suffering, calico chew-toy, Simon, his new big brother and guardian, and Jim Dandy, who loved everyone unconditionally, vehemently, and whether it was wanted or not.

Fatboy was slim enough to slip through the pen attached to the house. When I left Saturday afternoon, he was outside, setting about the serious business of frolicking with his buddies, Simon and Star, playing leapfrog, chasing leaves in the chaotic Kansas wind — a child of the sun enjoying his first spring.

I felt dread when I couldn't find him late Saturday night. All that night I called, *Fatboy! Fatboy Slim!* I kicked myself for leaving the window open to the pen. All Sunday I called, panic rising, *Fatman! Fatmandu!*

A spot of brilliant white caught my eye in the field, but I decided it was a sack or paper. It weighed heavy on me while I answered mail and worked on book jobs Sunday afternoon.

My heart nagged me to walk the field, look closer.

He laid there alone all night in the field off 7th and Prairie streets, so small against the country night sky — a victim of hit and run.

I carried him home, fallen warrior, beloved friend. He laid in-state in the backyard while I mustered the courage to dig his grave, to let go.

I found what I missed before — tire marks and brain matter on the curb near my house — and realize it wasn't an accident. He darted across the street and a long way into the field before he fell and died.

That exuberant rhythm is gone, that pudgy Taurus cat, that purring on my pillow, that stumbling up and down the stairs with a kitten under my feet.

I laid the remains of my fuzzy little familiar in his grave, covered him with a favorite green t-shirt, looked at Fatboy for the last time — and felt suddenly blessed.

I bless back.

I bless the cosmos for this rowdy, one-of-a-kind masterpiece and eight months of joy.

I bless those who hurt him and wish them no harm.

I bless the universe for balancing itself out.

I bless Fatboy's spirit and thank him for dropping in.

I welcome him to drop by again when he reincarnates, and assure him that love is always here, that love is always.

Flaming Orgasm

John, Rusty and I were at Kennedy's Claim,
enjoying draft beer,
since it was cheap and we were broke.

They were discussing various drinks
while I was lost somewhere in my own universe.
Rusty yelled, *Hey! Have you ever had
a 'flaming orgasm'?*

And I, startled back to reality,
said, *Well, I try ...*

FORE!

Some unknown neighbor
practices his swing –
golf balls litter my yard –
free cat toys

Friends in High Places

Mom and I usually went to Roadrunner Cafe
for a 3 a.m. dinner after working
on *Chiron* all evening at the *Tribune*.
One night there was a preppy young jerk
who snickered out loud at Mom's size.
It was months before I could convince
her to go back.

By that time, my best friend Rusty
began working there as a cook
on the late shift. On the night
I finally talked Mom into going
back, of course the jerk
was there in his usual booth
hateful and arrogant.

I whispered to Rusty,
*There's that butthead
who hurt Mom's feelings.*

Don't worry, said Rusty.
*Tell your mom
I spit on his cheeseburger.*

Your Forrest Gump

You come around all friendly and needy,
craving someone to fill the abyss –
nasty little pig all mean and greedy
looking for someone to take on the mess.

You run off half-cocked, ragged and mad,
into the unknown for whatever the ride,
then crawl back scratching at my screen door,
smelling like something that has died.

But I don't wanna be your Forest Gump!
I wanna be more than your Forest Gump!
I won't be your Forest Gump!

You come back around and use me up,
then take off running all over the world.
You say you love me all the while,
but you keep looking for that perfect girl.

You carry your pain like an invisible shield,
and bite off my head if I penetrate it.
You just won't yield to the love I wield,
no matter how I bait it!

But I don't wanna be your Forest Gump!
I wanna be more than your Forest Gump!
I won't be your Forest Gump!

You swallow any pill that you can grab
and screw whatever gets in your way,
and then you tell me I'm so drab
and you just can't wait to run away.

You drink and smoke but celebrate nothing,
and come home to me flat on your face,
gobbling salvation from my hand,
praying I'll heal your fall from grace.

But I don't wanna be your Forest Gump!
I wanna be more than your Forest Gump!
I won't be your Forest Gump!

From the Mouths of Babes

Rhonda and I were animal control officers,
chasing a weenie dog on foot
down an alley in a section of town
that was run-down,
dotted with mobile homes,
an area where people were murdered and raped,
but we were fearless
in pursuit of this delinquent animal.

The dog was frantic,
trying to keep ahead of us.

Half-way down the block in the middle of the alley,
was a young girl, five or six years old,
dirty dress, dirty face,
and wild, tangled hair.
The dog ran, cowered behind her legs
as the little raggedy girl,
standing firm, demanded, *What are you doing?*

*If you can't keep your dog tied up,
we'll have to take him in*, I said sternly.

With black eyes snapping, head tossed back,
hands on hips, she declared,
YOU DON'T RUN THE WORLD YOU KNOW!

She scooped up the frightened weenie dog
and walked away, her head high,
long hair slapping the wind.

FUCK POETRY!

i don't want to
write poems
anymore
(except this one)
bcz all the words
in the world have
already been used
and if i make up words
some old harpy
screams
rulesstructure!
rulesstructure!
at me til
i just say
oh fuck poetry
& go do some
thing else

The Gift

During this sleepless summer night
I may have found that thought
people think
right before suicide —
the one that makes suicide
inevitable.

I can't say what it is —
I wouldn't want to cause
anyone to *do it*.

Don't worry.
It doesn't inspire me to suicide.
It's okay with me that
oblivion is unavoidable.
I have no desire to fly in its face.

So oblivion is inevitable!
Oh well.

Seven kittens are playing out back,
tumbling over each other
in the moonlight.

Two calico mom cats look on
paws curled,
proud and content.

We are so damn lucky for little awhile.

God as Lover

On His bold body our black-eyed lover
wears the Past and the Future.
Intricately woven, hideous and pleasing,
it conforms gracefully
to every rough and gentle move.
Smooth and assured He moves
through the Present without panic,
without regrets.
He grins, slips out of it all.
It slides down His lean form
into a writhing mass at His feet.
He's so cool, so satisfying
in the most burning way.

untitled

God loves little
freaky guys
he plays jokes
& smashes
their empty mirrors
all the screaming
laughing pieces
he uses for
confetti   he
celebrates every
thing
he loves his
little freaky
guys he never
wants them to be
lonely he whispers
jokes at them he
tells them funny
funny secrets

Gross

I woke up in a pleasant mood
(highly unusual)
and settled down at the table
to enjoy my breakfast.

Two of my cats (Mudge & Tiny Dancer)
were crouched as usual on the table
just beyond reach of my only
defense weapon, a rolled-up copy of the
latest issue of *Cat Fancy* magazine.

(I allow them that small pleasure —
if they keep their distance
and mind their manners,
I will share with them.)

Mudge puked on the table
and I thought that was gross —
then Dancer ate it.

I left them the remainder
of my breakfast.

haiku-esque

the moon lingers in west
as sun peeks up in east —
God's tiny clocks

Hands

St. John Grade School, 1972

During 3rd grade, my best friend forever moved to Idaho. I was devastated. A new boy moved to town from Texas: good-natured, honest, a clown at heart & very real. The first time he smiled at me, my heart was his. Who knows how it started, but for two years we held hands in school every moment we were together. Until 5th grade, when Rebecca, a snotty high school teacher's aide saw us and sneered, *Boys do NOT hold hands!* She whacked our hands apart with her fist. Out of her sight, I reached for my friend's hand. He jerked it back. He walked away.

Great Bend, May, 1991

Robert and I were in the car on our first date. He was about to become my first serious lover. He reached for my right hand as I drove. I jerked away as if I'd been shot. He was hurt, and surprised as I was. I reached over, took his hand in mine. Held it the entire time I drove with the other. From then on, driving or walking, we were hand-in-hand, fingers locked against the crap of the world.

he holds me in such a way that shoves back the black hole of night
for Robert

By day he gives me constant static
and he's helping me grow my ulcer back,
but by night, no matter how much anger
we have exchanged,
he holds me and makes me laugh.
A lifetime of loneliness evaporates
and can no longer clutch my heart at 3 a.m.
He holds me in such a way that
shoves back the black hole of night.
He lightens my darkness with his luminous smile,
and keeps me laughing in a warm glow of love,
knowing that no matter how far apart
we get by day, by night
he'll be back in my bed, arms flung open
saying, *I'm here, I'm yours.*

About Heaven

If there are any heavens,
I'll get one —
not because my life was saintly,
or I did everything I *should* have done,
or didn't do what I *shouldn't* have done,
or believed a bunch of crap, or didn't —
but simply that every soul who suffers
this clumsy, tragic material mess
deserves a heaven.

I'd choose a simple heaven,
a small wood frame house way out in the country,
where it's always spring or autumn,
with rolling grass that is never mowed,
lots of trees in the distance
and a stream nearby.

The soul of every cat I ever knew will live there,
two rabbits named Melba and George,
two hens named Henny Penny and Penelope Beaker,
and five big rowdy dogs.

They'll all get along famously.
There will be no telephones, televisions or computers,
no automobiles or cowboys,
no religion, guns or money,

no sovereign boundaries,
no municipal laws or dreaded sickness,
no fleas or cat diseases.

There will be no people at all, except Mom
and a friend to visit now and then —
but they will be carefully screened —
and may not be
who they think they are.

How It Happens

The State declared him *disabled,*
but he is super smart and loves books and history.
He is dysfunctional in life and sorely awkward in social
    situations.
He doesn't fit anywhere
except somewhere on the Autism Spectrum.

In the harsh real world,
he isn't welcome too many places, not even family reunions —
but in the museum research library that I manage,
anyone who loves books is royalty.

He never approaches me, just goes straight to the books.
He's so near-sighted he holds the books
right up to his round granny specs to read.

His long hair is turning white.
He's big and round like Santa Claus.
He even dresses as Santa might dress at home
on the other 364 days —
perennial plaid, bright primary colors,
and the ever-present red suspenders.

He is eccentric, but so Victorian polite.
He seldom speaks, but when he does
it's with such earnestness,
such over-succinct enunciation.

His sentences are punctuated with pauses,
he pronounces each syllable
as if he invents the words as he speaks —
as if all creation hangs on a Word.

One
Morning

I was so much busier than usual in the library,
with researchers from other states,
and local folks researching genealogy.
Many scholars demanded assistance
as I rushed about in all the four directions.

He appeared in the midst of all this chaos,
and for the first time ever,
marched with purpose right up to my counter,
wearing an enigmatic, self-satisfied grin,
an omnipotent gleam in his eye.

With grand pomp and ceremony,
he held out an upturned fist,
and unfurled his fingers to reveal a perfect robin's egg.
For you, he said.

I thought, So this is how it happens.
Everyday-Santa just appears in the primordial void,
sporting John Lennon's specs and Mona Lisa's smile,
holds Brahmanda in the palm of his Orphic hand,
Pangu pops out
before you can even say *big bang.*

A Hug on Williams Street
Great Bend, Kansas, summer, 1993

He saw me downtown one sunny afternoon and followed me back to Connie's house where I was staying. He pulled up beside me and squealed his tires on the street, thinking it was impressing me, laid a black mark several feet long.

He yelled, *Hey! You trying to get away from me?*

I said, *Why would I want to get away from a handsome devil like you? I just didn't recognize you.*

He was about 5'8", thin, wiry, good-looking in a rough sort of way, with piercing brown Sagittarius eyes that could cut through any crap.

I really didn't recognize him at first— he'd let his hair grow out, had a new beard and was thinner — but he was still the handsome, macho, hyper, belligerent banty rooster who occasionally pursued me.

We sat on Connie's porch and made small talk for awhile. Then he said, *I need to talk to Jon.*

Sorry. I can't tell you where he is. He has someone new and doesn't want to see you.

Do you know why I need to talk to him?

Yes. Jon already knows. We all do.

His eyes darted around. He put his hands in his pockets, shifted around on his feet, weighed his words.

It's true. I am. He looked at me intensely, watching for my reaction.

He started walking toward his car. I followed. The words poured out:

I'm surprised you didn't run away. Aren't you afraid of me now? You wouldn't believe the fuckin' shit people say, what they do.

My girlfriend's family won't let me stay at their house anymore; her brother won't teach me karate anymore and I've been taking from him for two years! None of my friends will have anything to do with me. No one wants to even touch me anymore! Are you afraid of me? It makes me so goddamn mad! I don't want to die. I'm only 33 goddamn years old! The nurse showed me a film of what's going to happen to me — I'll get these big goddamn purple sores, I'll look like a skeleton ... I feel fine now! I just can't believe it. I used a condom every time. Why couldn't they have done the same for me? I don't even know who gave it to me. But I want to kill someone. So I like to have sex with guys. Do I have to die because of it? I'm embarrassed to even be talking about it.

His anger filled the air. His pain was tangible. There were no words that could make things better. He paced in the street, still watching my reactions, edging closer and closer to his car, waiting for rejection, getting ready for his escape.

I finally managed, *I liked you when I first met you and that is not going to change. Don't be embarrassed to be human ...* I offered him my hand.

I saw a tear on his arrogant macho face, a glimmer of hope in his eyes. He took my hand, then threw his arms around me, pressed against me in a ferocious bear hug. I wrapped my arms around him and held him as tight as I could. With his head against my chest, my face buried in his hair, I stood there in the middle of the street holding him as words continued to elude me, as if just holding him could cure him; as if I could squeeze the virus right out of him; as if I was stronger than death.

I murmured, *I wish there was something I could do ... I don't know what to say ... Come back and see me, okay?*

Wiping tears from his eyes, he smiled and said, *Okay.*

Minutes later he was peeling out of there like a maniac, a wild animal in pain, desperate to escape from himself.

i wish i'd met Antler when i was 13

anyboy would be cosmically lucky to spend two months
wandering the wilderness alone with Antler: exploring,
discovering the unsingable virtues of nature. learning
he's been buried under layers and layers of lies. anyboy
might learn that two boys achieving mutual joy is
more manly more godly more Christ-like than mutual
annihilation. anyboy might learn to swat Baptists like
mosquitoes. anyboy might learn not to be terrified of
himself, of his ability to love. anyboy might not be eaten
by ulcers in 9th grade. anyboy might learn he was born a
legitimate child of the universe. as much as cottonwoods,
buffaloes, meadowlarks, sunflowers, as much as air, dirt,
grass, stars.

i'm not a punching bag but ...

ratboy is stronger than me
and likes to hit
it is an art.
his eyes dilate,
his face gets a hard mean look,
he doubles his fist and swings wide,
brown biceps bulge

i like it,
the way it jars my whole being
that thud on my arm
or leg, or back, once in the eye
(you really do see stars)

the sheer male power behind the punch.
i never had that power,
it mystifies, eludes me.

i like seeing it, feeling it,
understanding it

i take his touch, his skin
any way he offers it

It's Been Said Peace Begins In Your Own Back Yard
5:30 a.m., March 27, 1999

People in Kosovo are fleeing
their own homes, being murdered,
even as I listen to the radio,
safe in the middle of Kansas.

I step outside, check on the wild cats,
fix them warm farm milk, two cans of 9 Lives,
two big bowls of Science Diet dry.

I fight the Kansas March wind
to fix a blanket atop the cellar door
where they huddle under two board planks
leaning against my house;

put a blanket over the boards,
put heavy plastic over that;
weight it down with bricks,
buckets, shovels and boards.

I hold Orange Son in my arms —
he's a year old, slightly tame and very fluffy —
pet him gently, speaking softly,
simple words like *love* and *sacred gift* —

until his purring is louder than the wind;

make them all as safe and warm and content
as a poor poet can —

give them whatever peace I have.

Judgment Day

once, in the middle of a
rowdy motel room encounter
with a very flexible guy named Bob
and a bottle of Jim Beam,
I remembered what the preacher shouted,
red-faced
at the top of his lungs
in the Baptist church of my childhood.

On Judgment Day,
YOU will stand before GAWD
& every person who ever lived on earth,
including YOUR family & friends,
and YOUR life with be replayed
on a giant screen in front of YOU
like a MOVIE for ALL to see!

I stop.
Flash a big smile,
wave to the camera,
say, *Hi Mom!*

Kerouac's Gotta be Hiding Around Here Somewhere!

I.
One night in April,
Connie, John and I stepped into the small
Missionary Baptist Church to visit Freida
who was hired to paint a mural
on the back wall of the full-immersion baptistery.

Freida painted and ignored us,
standing in the baptistery barefoot
where a couple of inches of water remained.
I played hymns on the piano
while Connie and John sang.
Then we all gathered in the choir seats
to talk at Freida while she created.

Connie said, *Did I tell you about Victoria?*
Then her eyes rolled heavenward,
... Oh, I can't. It involves s-e-x.

John said, *God can spell, Connie.*

Freida stopped painting and turned to us.
She leaned over the waist-high glass splash-guard
in her Dolly Parton wig,
lit a cigarette, cat eyes gleaming
and with a devilish grin said,
I'm smokin' in holy water!

II.
Connie and I were bored and at large
on the streets of Great Bend, Kansas
looking for friends to invade.
As we drove by the Jayhawker Motel
we remembered our friend
the fire-haired, green-eyed imp/angel
Victoria Delilah
had checked in there recently
to live for awhile.

We parked and knocked on #14 around midnight.
After a few moments, Victoria opened the door
smiling and hugged us while clutching
a skimpy nightgown to her ample bosom.

Against the backdrop
of a Motley Crüe tapestry on one wall
and an American flag on the other,
she invited us in to her here and now.
It was then we noticed
through the gray smoke haze
and the television's blue glow
two half-dressed, handsome teen-age boys
laughing and rough-housing
each other in her bed.

We offered to leave
but Victoria, eyes twinkling,
said, *No! Stay!*

She leaned over the desk
and lit her cigarette from a candle
burning atop a steer skull.
She grinned, face glowing:
So how is my favorite poet?

Last Supper
for Jean

I always thought death would be dramatic.
I knew she was dying of cancer
but had never seen anyone die, much less painfully.
I thought she would fight, struggle and gasp for breath.
I thought someone would hold her hand.
I thought she'd be in a hospital bed with IVs
instead of hunched over in a chair,
with her pain pills being rationed.
I thought she might even avoid it somehow
and rise laughing at us all.

I had hoped perhaps we would have
a poignant bedside conversation
and forgive each other a 12-year-old altercation
for harsh words that were thought and spoken.

She just said, *I'd like a Tootsie Roll & an apple.*
So I drove to the Quik Shop and got her
a Tootsie Roll and an apple.
She said, *Thank you Mike,*
and ate the Tootsie Roll after mom cut it up for her.

She died quietly three hours later.

The last I saw of her she was slumped
in her chair, dead at three o'clock in the morning,

no fanfare, no angels, no trumpets,
no mighty struggle, no gasping.

After three years, she simply and gladly
surrendered to the pain.

Leapfrog

Ratboy & I drove to Lawrence
to hear Lesléa Newman speak at KU.
Lesléa is a writer who would later appear
on the cover of *Chiron Review*.

On our way to the classroom where she was to speak,
I said to Ratboy, *I wonder if Fred Phelps will be here?*
A bloated red-faced bearded man walking near us snapped,
Damn STRAIGHT he'll be here!
as he puffed up and swaggered away from us.

It should have gone without saying that
America's vile and caustic homophobic bigot —
the disbarred lawyer and Baptist preacher
who protested the funerals of gay men who died of AIDS,
who protested little Ryan White's funeral,
who faxed a drawing to President Clinton
of his mother burning in hell the day she died —
would be there with bells on to protest Lesléa's visit.

Lesléa was the most banned author of the 1990s,
author of *Heather Has Two Mommies* —
a childrens' book about a little girl
being raised by two lesbian moms.

As fans visited with Lesléa before her program,
we heard some loud, excited voices outside.
We moved to the window
to see what the commotion was on the ground
three stories below.

And there they were,
surrounded by a circle of protective policemen:
Fred Phelps' and his congregation,
faces contorted, wielding protest signs,
screaming at intellectual gay-friendly students
who were attempting to reason with them.

The protestors yelled their typical names & epithets
at gay couples who held hands, kissed,
and made out with each other
just to bait them.

Fred's wife stood on a soapbox,
her big church lady hair reaching towards Heaven.
She held a frightened shivering wiener dog,
and sang "Amazing Grace" at the top of her lungs.

Fred's teen-aged son held a crude sign,
depicting male stick figures engaging in anal sex.

Lesléa said, *Is all that for me?*
Yes, I said with a smile, *Aren't you lucky?*
Fred Phelps came out just for you!

A bubbly effeminate gay KU student
spied Fred Jr.'s crude stick figure sign,
put his hands on his hips and said bemusedly,
*Hmmm … it appears the faggots
are playing leapfrog!*

Letting Go

Dear Robert Cooperman,
I spilled coffee on your poems.
It wasn't just: la la la, sitting at the desk,
drinking coffee, opening mail,
& oops! spilled coffee all over the manuscripts!
No, it had to be like this:
my aunt died –
my aunt who was really my mom
since her big sister died 15 years ago to the day.
We are in the process of clearing out her house,
my brother, sister and I.
It's just across the street from my house.
On Saturday mornings, I loved to roll out of bed,
stumble over to her house with my coffee,
watch *In the Heat of the Night* with her,
play with her rambunctious kittens.
More often than not, she'd make breakfast.
She kept a big bowl of peanut M&Ms on the kitchen table for me.
I wasn't supposed to have them, but we reasoned
the protein in the peanuts balanced the sugar in the chocolate.
That bowl was never empty.
Did I already say she was more than an aunt?
That she was my neighbor and best friend
who helped generously and often with kitty & *Chiron* chores;
that every time I look across the street at her empty house
it's like a punch in the gut?

She loved pink flamingos. In my Florida travels,
I bought her kitschy pink flamingo souvenirs and post cards
for taking care of my super-sized clowder while I was gone.
She left eight cats, so now I have eight more cats —
eight promises are eight promises.
So it was a Saturday morning, eight days after her death.
I stumbled out to get the mail,
clutching my grown-up sippy-cup of coffee.
I grabbed the mail from the box, it included your poetry submission.
I spied the two pink flamingos that adorned my aunt's front yard,
looking so forlorn and all askew from the Kansas wind,
and decided it was time to bring them home.
I crossed the street and stupidly stuffed the cup of coffee &
mail in my big parka pocket together.
One of the flamingo's wire legs was missing.
As I remember it, I leaned to look for the all-important piece of
wire and stumbled to my knees and felt the coffee spill in my pocket.
An on-looker might have said, *That guy was just standing there,
staring down at some cheap-ass plastic pink flamingos
and his knees just buckled!*
That was how I spilled coffee all over a poetry submission
for the first time in 33 years, and Bob, I was so sorry,
I knelt at those flamingos and just cried.

Lions 1, Christians 0

I glanced out my bedroom window in time to see Dancer, my 11-year-old, 14-pound yellow cat, hopping out of the preacher's brand new convertible mazda miata at the church across the street. I was horrified, knowing Dancer's territorial ideology, knowing from experience those unholy things he does to the insides of cars when the windows are left down. I ran frantically downstairs, flung open the door and called him. I wanted him home, before he had to learn about the Christian obsession with retribution, what Christians do to those who do what comes natural. He pranced and danced home, pleased with himself. I smiled, *Ba-a-a-ad kit-ty!* and fed him a whole can of his favorite food.

Love Light

Their marriage was based
on mutual hatred and greed.
Neither wanted to split the assets,
so they stayed together.

Their reward was
all manner of ill health
and ulcers.

Camilla began working at love.
She read new age books
about forgiveness, letting go
and love energy.

She said, *The book said
I should visualize a pink aura
around him.
"Pink" light is "love" light.
But I just can't imagine that!
So instead, I imagine him
floating in a pool
of Pepto-Bismal.*

me and rhonda on astronomy & humanitarianism
corner of Forest & Williams, Great Bend, Ks., October, 1985

standing outside the Chinese restaurant, having just eaten dinner after seeing *Godzilla '85*, arguing how gross shrimp tails are or are not: i could not fathom how anyone could bear to have one on a plate & retain a healthy appetite. she had performed a puppet show with them for me. the shrimp danced & sang, *if you lived in Ethiopia, you would just love love love us!* i looked up to see Halley's Comet once before it left. the whole point of our date being for her to help me see the comet once as it crossed paths with my tiny life. i had no clue where to look, the sky being infinite & all. she said, *it's the little twinkling thing.* i noted everything up there was twinkling its little heart out. she said, *by Jupiter.* i asked, *where the hell is Jupiter? remember who can't find his way to Kansas City.* her usual benevolent frustrated sigh. *above Steinert's Furniture. the big brilliant dot is Jupiter, below: the comet spinning on its axis. stare at it awhile. it has a tail, a brief wisp of light. it's traveling thousands and thousands of miles a minute.* wow. will it ever crash to earth? who knows? if so i hope it lands on Ethiopia as i'm ever so tired of that damn song. i thought Godzilla took care of that. no, that was Japan. oh. well, let them eat shrimp!

Melba's Cocktail

Every time we took a shopping trip
to Great Bend, Melba asked me
to stop at Hejny's Liquor Store
on the way out of town.

I helped her up the steps
with her complaining about
the lack of a handrail,
though she was spry for 90.

She looked around the store,
asked questions about the different liquors,
but always settled on six bottles
of Popov or Smirnoff vodka.

The clerk rang them up.
As Melba wrote her check, she explained,
I have a little cocktail
every night with my salad,
just a medicine cupful in some fruit juice.
The Mayo Clinic told me to do this
to relax me once a day, so it's medical.
It's deductible.

message

tell God i would
trade my saturday shirt
for a peek through the
crack in His basement floor
or 1/2 a glimpse of His face
or just an eye
if He would only look me
in the eye
i promise not to
glow

moon babies

we ride the spirit
that moves us
into a funny universe.
i kiss
the stardust from his
silly smile.
eat his deepest
sleep / let him
awaken slowly in me.
do ragtime on
his hot keyboards.
kamikaze into his
coolcat dreams.
make him laugh.
grow fields of love
in his arid heart,
drink his timid trust.

Letter to Mother, 7 Years Later, Postmarked Home

Today was the seventh anniversary of your passing. It seems impossible that you've been gone that long; that it's been seven years since I've had a conversation or an argument with you, a long ride around town in the middle of the night. But what seems most impossible is that I survived and adjusted so well to your absence. I guess the human spirit is amazingly resilient, even mine. We have more power within us than we ever realize. Who knew?!? But it has been hard.

It was a terrible night that started with a phone call at one o'clock a.m. I was just leaving The Page with Lee Ann and Shon. Cousin Connie called my cell phone to say you'd gone by ambulance to the hospital. I rushed to the hospital, 45 minutes away, as fast as I could, but it was the longest drive of my life. Shon might have driven, I don't remember.

You lived 19 hours after that. Aunt Charlene stayed with you the whole time. I wasn't able to do so, and I apologize for that. I took a couple of breaks and went home to care for cats and gather my wits (which were no where to be found). Somewhere inside, I knew you were dying, but still I kept thinking you'd pull through, because you always had before.

Due to your low oxygen count, you were unable to match your thoughts to the right words. None of what you said made sense, though you were able to understand what people said to you. You were always able to say, *I love you.* You said it to every member of your extended family who came to visit.

That Sunday afternoon, your sisters and brother as well as many nephews and nieces came to the hospital to say what I realize now were their good-byes. They stayed until that evening, but eventually, it was only Charlene, Connie, Sally, Shon and I in the room. About five p.m., a nurse gave you morphine. You fell in to a deep sleep. Your suffering ended then, but you hung onto life for almost six more hours. Charlene, who was a CNA, knew when the heart monitor beeped irregularly. She said softly, *It's time*. We gathered around your bed and took turns holding your hands. As life left your body, we stood there helplessly, escorted you off this planet as best we could.

Watching you die was hard enough, but even harder was gathering your belongings from the hospital room and putting them in the backseat of the car, going in to your empty house in the middle of the night. I stepped in the front door of the house I had grown up in. Sitting on the back of the sofa was our cat Buddy, a gentle blue/gray cat who was five at the time. I dropped the sack with your things. Your shoes spilled onto the floor. I stared at your shoes as the realization you would never need them again sunk in. Buddy looked at me with that beatific, loving, knowing look cats have. My knees buckled. I collapsed on the couch, threw my arms around Buddy and burst into uncontrollable sobs. I don't know if that lasted a long time or a short time, but it is the only time I remember completely losing control. Buddy didn't struggle to get away from me, and it must have been such a frightening spectacle to him. But he continued purring and let me lay there with my face buried in his soft fur as long as I needed to. You would have been proud of him.

Your death occurred in the middle of a 10-year span in which I had no spiritual belief system. I was in a nihilistic/atheistic place that was working for me at the time. It's interesting that I coped with and survived your passing without any spiritual belief system. Many people either get religion or lose it during a time like this, but your passing didn't influence my belief system either way. I coped by throwing myself into work. Keeping busy was the best therapy.

There were also a handful of friends – Aunt Charlene, Sister Sal, Lee Ann, Rusty and Dawn – who *baby-sat* me and kept tabs on me, spent time with me and made sure I didn't sink into despair. There were also Shon and Amber, who had planned to move out of my house, but postponed a move to stay nearby until they knew I'd be okay.

But not a day goes by that I don't miss you terribly. Most people find anniversaries and holidays to be difficult, but I don't. It's the everyday things ... your favorite songs on the radio, a flash of bright yellow, the phone ringing and realizing it can't be you. This doesn't just happen on Feb. 20, holidays or any special anniversary, it happens every day. Even so, it isn't a debilitating pain, just a sudden pang, a void that will always be there. Like dear Virginia said, *Sorrow is a granite slab I hug against my dead heart. The only remedy is to bear it.**

Grief becomes a part of you, something you almost cherish and nurture but don't over-indulge. It is something that becomes bearable with time. I keep my grief shut behind a door and only allow it to come out once in a while. Of course, sometimes that door flies wide open on its own.

You were my best friend. I know it isn't *cool* for a guy to admit his mother was his best friend, but you were. If there is such a thing as reincarnation, and I'm thinking maybe there is,

I feel we had many lives together. We were more than parent/child. We were soulmates. We were so different in so many ways, but the bond between us was epic. Small-minded, petty people would say I was just a *Mama's Boy*. But it was so much more than that.

I didn't get along so well with you growing up, you were Mother first, Friend, second. Our friendship happened after I grew up and learned to appreciate you for the person you were in your own right, not just as *Mike and Joe's Mom* or *Jerry's Wife*.

We became best friends, and I don't see anything wrong with that. I think it is a beatific thing when a parent and child can overcome their issues in one lifetime and become best friends. It's no easy task. No simple/small-minded people manage it. No self-centered, petty people manage it. No weak people manage it. It takes real give and take; of loving and forgiving; of downright hard work and soul-searching; of just letting go.

It would have been so much harder if I'd had terrible regrets, but I don't. We talked about our *issues* calmly. The negative issues I had with you dissipated long before you passed on. I also realized early on that you did the very best you could with what you knew and how you were taught; that you dealt with serious illness most of my growing up years and that would naturally color those years; that most issues were insignificant.

It's too easy to get bogged down in the negative, in the mistakes. I let go of them. I dwelt on the positive, happy times from my childhood through adulthood, and there were many. I dwelt on the fact that I never had to doubt for one second that my siblings and I were cherished.

I just enjoyed your company while I could. I'm so glad. It could have been so much worse.

There are, of course, things I wish I'd done differently, some things I didn't say that I assume went without saying, but wish I'd said anyway. But it's finished. I feel good about those last few years.

You loved being included in my life, being a part of my friends' lives, being accepted and adored in our little circle. No one realized how lonely and shut out you felt most of your life. You loved being part of *Chiron Review* and the poetry activities. It made you feel a part of something vital and living, that you had found your kindred spirits.

Three weeks after you passed on, I was hired to work at the museum. The job saved my sanity. It was something I could throw myself into. The cataloging, the organizing, the creating, as well as working on *Chiron* and taking care of the cats at home, kept my brain and body busy (and the bills paid) while my heart went on auto-pilot for several years.

Frazier went off the air. I remember how much you loved that show. I remembered how once, when you were sick, you taped an episode with one of *Niles*' solo bits, that you re-wound and watched that skit over and over. You hee-hawed and laughed harder and harder each time. If laughter really is the best medicine, David Hyde Pearce must have bought you at least an extra year or two!

I moved back home three years ago. It's not the same without you and Dad and the kids underfoot – too quiet – but the walls do talk. The memories and love are tangible.

Your cats are glad I'm back. They were living semi-feral outside since you left and had a couple of rough winters. Out of our 30 combined cats, Jackie Brown was the only one whose name you could recall and say in the delirium of your final hours. When you managed to say, *Jackie* ... I knew you wanted me to promise I'd take care of her and all the cats, and I did make that promise, and have kept it.

Since you left, some new cats have moved in and found sanctuary here. This is your on-going legacy – shelter for the homeless, food for the hungry, love for everyone, no one turned away, human or animal. Your attitude always made me think of some of those red letters in the Bible: What you do for the least of these, you do for Me.

Some of the older cats have passed on: Nick, Robin, Dancer, Christine, Cecilia, Jack, Ekin, Joni, Fatboy, Big Mama Naomi, Bukowski ... I miss them, but I like to think you met them at the threshold of eternity with open arms, are keeping them company now, or perhaps guided them gently to their next appointment.

Their passing was heartbreaking, but even as they left, new friends were making their way to my home. I would love for you to meet Angel, Frankie, Roxanne, Dylan Thomas, Rocky, Harley, Cornelius, Apollonia, Charlie, Oliver, Alice, Clown, Shorty, Nigella and her family.

In October 2002, someone shot Stormy in the left eye. Two days went by without anyone seeing him on the property, which was unoccupied at the time. We didn't think much about it, but on the third day, I went looking for him. I saw a black lump in a corner on the back porch. I thought he was dead. He was alive, but couldn't move. His head was bleeding. I picked up him, put him in the car and drove like a maniac to the vet, calling ahead on my cell phone.

Our vet said someone had shot Stormy in the eye with a .22. His right eye was ruined and his jaw was fractured. I didn't think he'd make it, since he was almost 10, and had lain there for at least two days, injured, without food and water. I said, *I assume all we can do is him put to sleep?* The vet said, *He could make it.* So I said, hope taking glorious flight, *Oh yes, then do what you can!* And that scrapper pulled through! It shouldn't have surprised me, remembering the life of abuse and torment he survived before you and Dad rescued him in the summer of 1993. Within a week, he was back home, eating, purring, being the big old affectionate goofball that he is. Aunt Charlene and I decided he couldn't live outside anymore, so she let him move into her guest room. She takes good care of him. Knowing how much you loved that goofy old cat, and how much he loved you, I think it makes us feel that part of you is still with us, albeit looking at us through one eye.

A week before your passing, you asked me to take care of Aunt Charlene but you acknowledged it works in reverse with her. Her commitment to caring for others is only outdone by her fierce independence.

I promised to look after Joe and Karen but was unable to save them from themselves. All I could do was back off and let them fall. Seven years later, they both seem to be finding their way back. You would be proud of them for that, but if you had survived your last illness, their shenanigans would have finished you off for sure.

I cleaned out the cellar, found the old suitcase with my sister Kristi's clothes and funeral things, that suitcase you shoved into the furthest, darkest place you could find more than 40 years ago. I dealt with it the best I could. I threw out the once-dainty clothes the mice ruined; read, for the first time in my adult life, that bundle of old cards and letters from family and friends, that outpouring of love, grief and support, not one word of which ever lifted you from that far, dark place.

I put those cards and letters, along with Kristi's baby book, her bottle, shoes and pink rattle – those painful talismans you could not bear to see even one more time – in Grandma's cedar chest. I wish there were more I could have done. But it is the most I can do, to continue holding her memory sacred, to tell you one last time her sickness and death were not your fault. Precious few babies survived spinal meningitis back then, and if any mother could have brought her through it, it would have been you.

For all the grief and sorrow you endured, something happened a year and three months after you passed that I truly believe would have wiped it all away in one cleansing fell swoop. On May 25, 2001, your first grandson, Seth, was born to Joe and his wife. Seth is handsome and bright. His eyes are alight with curiosity and an excited, ever-growing quest for knowledge and understanding. He has a zest for life that he must have inherited directly from you. And he talks too much and too loud – just like everyone in our family always has. I'd like to have a nickel for every time he is going to hear the phrase, *Let's use our "inside" voices.* How you would love this rowdy, vibrant child!

How you would love our family gatherings with the boisterous shenanigans of Seth and your other grandchildren, Kristi, Lucas and Alyssa! They are such lively little people. Sometimes when I'm watching them play, I think of how proud you would be, how joyfully you would have embraced each one of them, how eagerly they would have returned your love. Their faces are so bright, four little smiling suns rising just for us to light the terrible darkness left at your passing.

Though your final words were gibberish, I know exactly what you were trying to say. I could see it in your frantic eyes, your last answer to that debate we'd had just a week before you left – about an afterlife. You were trying to say that this deathbed good-bye would not be final; that love never dies even if our bodies do. You wanted to reach me for just one moment in my soul's *dark night* to say that in spite of my logic and doubt, you believed in the Everlasting; that somehow in ways we cannot even fathom, we will be together again; that you needed for me to believe that, just long enough for both of us to let go. For what it's worth, I believe it now.

* Virginia Love Long, "Casting of the Stones," from *Squaw Winter,* Kindred Spirit Press, 1987.

My New Career

Some call him handicapped, some call him *special,* some call him mentally disabled. I imagine he's been called worse in his 59 years. I just call him Slim. I work for him midnight to eight a.m., clean his house, see to it he has safe, peaceful sleep. Around seven he hobbles out of bed, appears in his living room doorway, what little hair he has standing at-attention. With his near-toothless grin he says, *HI!!! ... I'm hu-u-u-n-n-n-n-ngy!* While I fix his cereal, he shuffles around his bedroom donning t-shirt and overalls. He pats my shoulder, sits down to eat, says, *Thank you, Man.* He shovels frosted flakes in his mouth, too fast, milk dribbling down his chin. He approaches me at the sink, so earnestly, nose-to-nose. He wants to tell me he's finished eating through a mouthful of un-chewed cereal, but coughs unexpectedly. There I stand laughing at shift's end, my face a puddle of milk and soggy frosted flakes.

The Mad Housesitter Has a Good Day

Coffee's dripping into this
day without clocks.
Nobody wants me.
I can listen to echoes all morning,
talk informally with the turtle
in Amber's flower garden,
share wheat crackers & popcorn,
Write Dear Suzanne without hurry-up,
tell her about this clockless day,
how the cat's asleep in the breadbox,
how something is right
with the world.

me & ratboy run the gamut of literary lovers

sometimes we're jack & neal,
poking & challenging
each others' minds & histories,
entire belief systems
in motel rooms & cars
with no destinations

drunken thoughts & words roll
across the black manuscript
of strange city night skies

we move & run
as if our lives depend upon it.

sometimes i am
ginsberg & williams
& he is nameless tasty chicken.
i beg him
to let me help every inch
of his long brown body
into heaven

sometimes we are auden & kallman.
i hate him for being young.
i hate him for being in love
with the whole world.
i hate the whole world
for being in love with him.

but he is most at ease
when we are Beavis & Butt-head,
stuck in small Kansas towns
with no money,
punching each other,
biting each other,
exploring the taste of blood,
the art of pain,
creating fat purple bruises
on the canvas of our bodies.

Medicare for All

That little phrase flies in the face
of Ayn Rand's Gospel of Selfishness,
causes the bauble-heads of conservative extremists
to spin in 360 degree circles,
squawking *Socialism!* like hysterical stuck records.

They sneer *Socialism!* like it's a bad thing,
as if it doesn't make sense,
as if isn't a rational balance,
a happy medium between the two harmful extremes
of Communism and Capitalism,

as if it isn't common sense compassion,
taking care of our families, friends and neighbors,
regardless of cost.

as if the word *business* or *profit*
should ever be associated with any vocation
holding human life, suffering and death
in the palm of its hand,

as if the free market isn't God,
as if there aren't more important things than money,
as if it isn't throwing the money-grubbers
out of the temple.

Midwesterner's Prune Face (MPF)
[aka Bible-Belter's Prune Face (BBPF)]

I'm no doctor or scientist, but I've noticed this until-now un-named disease prevalent in the midwest — especially predominant in adults who practice organized religion, and insecure heterosexual men.

I've caused so many outbreaks of it myself, I took the liberty of naming it.

It is triggered by casual contact with other humans who the MPF sufferer dislikes or disapproves of on sight for any reason, real or imagined; or feels superior to morally, physically, financially or spiritually, and is obligated (for the good of all decent humanity) to manifest that disgust.

Most recent case study:

My mom, roommate Ratboy and I visited an eatery in Stafford, Kansas. Mom and I were used to the mild cases of MPF the cashier suffered each Sunday when we patronized the quaint cafe. Maybe the weekly sight of a thirtysomething queer vegetarian poet having the nerve to even exist, much less hang out with and enjoy the company of his big, bold and beautiful vegetarian poet mom in the middle of Bob Dole's Kansas triggered it, and no attempts at friendliness or humor could cure it or relieve the symptoms ...

But add to the concoction a long-haired, hyperactive, mouthy teen-ager wearing a Marilyn Manson t-shirt proclaiming, *I AM THE GOD OF FUCK* in large slut-red letters, and there you have the formula for disaster: the most dire case of MPF in history.

The tragic result was a helpless midwestern Christian woman contorting her face in all manner of ways, desperate to register her disapproval, eyes bugging out, trying to bore a hole through the teen-ager's head to transmit her rage.

The disease was only exacerbated by The God of Fuck's sincere disinterest in her illness. He breezed through the entire dining experience, oblivious to her gross disease.

You Know You're Loved When People Are Willing to Give You the Moon

It was a late evening on North Boston Street in Stafford, Kansas, summer of 1964. I was three, Mom held me, smiling, pointing up to a full moon which seemed to be resting not that far away on the horizon. She said, *Isn't it pretty?* and I said, *Yeah, Daddy's gonna get me that to play with!*

***

In the autumn of 1995, I was dazed and befuddled at the tail-end of a wild three-year love that had picked my heart and soul clean. I gave all I had to this boy who would leave in the winter. There was no animosity, it was just done.

Our last outing was to a flea market on my late September birthday. When we were done looking, I went on to the car while he stayed behind to talk with friends.

I watched his long-legged saunter to the car. With that smile that never failed to melt me into a puddle of boneless goo, he hands me my first and only present – a globe of Earth's moon and says, *You should have **this**.*

***

It was a typical festive autumn evening, 1991, at my crowded Stone Street house. There was something going on in every corner, talking, laughing, some smoking and drinking ... but it wasn't a party, it was just that all five residents of the house had company.

Victoria Delilah and I were on the east end of the oversized living room, perched comfortably in Victorian chairs, our backs to the big picture window facing Roosevelt Junior High. We visited animatedly with Connie Star about everything under (and over) the sun, teasing her unmercifully because she was ordering everyone around, *Bring me this, get me that.*

Sylvia, the young brindle calico Connie gave me, lunged into the room carrying a steel wool scratcher in her mouth.

Connie demanded, *Somebody **get** that – she's gonna **kill** herself!*

We said, *She's okay – don't be such a mother hen!* Connie sprung all 250 pounds of her mother hen self into action, darted from the chair and chased Ms. Sylvia down, confiscating the steel wool sponge.

Victoria and I exclaimed in disbelief in our most dramatic evangelical voices: *It's a miracle! She can walk! Her legs are no longer broken! Praise be to Gawd, it's a miracle!*

Connie darted that sharp, green-eyed look, tossed her long red hair, turned her back to us, bent over and planted her thumbs in the elastic band of those plum purple stretch pants. Before we could save ourselves, down went those polyester pants and up came the fullest moon that ever rose on Great Bend, Kansas.

moon-in-aquarius

like you,
i am tame, civilized in public,
usually in private.
but i don't take it
as seriously as you do
i know it isn't natural

do you ever get sick of always
doing the right thing?
don't you ever get tired of
perfection and the pure wonderfulness
of it all? don't you ever get bored
with striving to always be
first, best, top?

isn't there a sneering,
drooling, primal creature
lurking inside you,
needing to break out
(just sometimes)
to destroy the carefully balanced
law of it all,
the practiced protected tradition
by centuries of bland,
frightened humanity?

don't you ever want to go blazing
into the forests & fields on Sept. 1
with a gun in each hand
like Yosemite Sam
screaming, *Sport THIS, Sportsmen!*

don't you ever want to go
on a Carry Nation rampage,
destroying every television set,
cell phone and computer
in the world?

to say *MOTHERFUCKER*
out loud in church

don't you ever want to
hurl yourself naked
off the top of a huge skyscraper
or mountaintop

searching for meaning,
for absolute anarchy?

(me neither)

moonlight dance

In the 10th grade,
he liked me because I was
smart and quiet and always
did the right thing.
I liked him because he had
long legs; because he had a
crazy wild-ass spirit;
because being near him made me
feel warm and weak in the knees.

On a Friday night
just before school was out
for summer,
we each snuck out of our houses
to be together.
We walked, found ourselves
on the edge of town.
We had so much to say,
we couldn't talk.
We walked in that bloated silence
until he let out a warhoop,
started running, clawing
at his clothes.
He pulled off his t-shirt and jeans.
flung them into the embracing darkness.
I watched him run and dance,
naked in moonlight.

night problem

i whisper to
blind shadows
begging them to
laugh
or open their
fat black eyes

but

all they do
is hang there
waiting
for sun to
spit morning
at their faces

The Non-Smoker's Right

At our parties, alcohol flowed,
music, laughter and all kinds of smoke
billowed out every window.

After she quit her own 30-year habit,
Connie complained loudly of the smoke
at these parties ...
until the time she whined,

Do you have to smoke?!?
It makes it hard to breathe!

Rusty took a puff on his cigarette,
looked her dead in the eye
and said, *Then don't.*

note to a sleeping guy

i've gotta run, but
i washed your shirts
they're in your drawer.
Emily got through her kitty surgery,
she has to have big ole
horse pills twice daily.
there's leftover pizza in the fridge
for when you wake up,
beer too.
a pack of cigs on my desk.
i miss our night-long talks.
i miss talking period.
the silence has descended
like a hateful fog.
you won't talk,
snap my head off when i try.
i survived oral surgery yesterday
had a bad wisdom tooth removed.
what hurts
i cut out
& leave behind.

Ode to Grandpa Hathaway
for Willie Roberts Hathaway, 1913-1996

he died of a stroke today, age 83, in his favorite chair
at home. his youngest grandchild playing at his feet.
grandma puttering around the house. no symptoms. no
warnings. no lingering, no nursing home. just the blink
of an eye. could anyone ask for more than that?

he was a loud cranky funny hillbilly farmer. he ignored
church. the good ladies of the First Missionary Baptist
Church in St. John, America were convinced (praise
Gawd!) he was headed for hell in a handbasket

i wasn't real close to him but like to think i inherited some
word-slinging talent from him. i pondered this the day i
walked into his house just in time to hear him shout

HOLY GOD DAMN SHIT ON THE EARTH!

i figured only a true poet could string a phrase like that.

One of Cassandra's, er, I Mean Mother's Dire Prophecies Actually Comes True

Some day one of those hitchhikers you pick up will be a murderer!
– Elsie Jane Hathaway, summer, 1988

I first saw him in that November dream,
his gaunt skin, sickness of spirit, intense Scorpio eyes.
I felt his desire to kill, and his loneliness

Maybe I spent those summer nights
searching the city for him,
knowing he would be there on midnight streets,
walking and watching for me.

As I drove up beside him, he turned.
I asked, *Can I give you a ride?*

He said, *I don't know you,*
and got into my car.

We drove around all night.
As the story of his broken life poured out,
he never took his eyes off the road ahead.

By the light of the dashboard,
he spoke of the abuse he suffered at the hands of his father,
the abuse he witnessed his mother suffer;
of a hatred that grew stronger as he grew stronger;

of rage, murder and prison;
of madness that had haunted his 22 years;
of fights he's been in and everyone who ever hurt him.

He warned me, *You don't mess with a Scorpio.*
You can tell when I'm mad —
it's almost always when there is no moon.
You just leave when I'm mad.
I don't want to hurt you.

He didn't scare me.
He spoke of parties, pranks and mooning cops;
of sex in the back room at the country club where he works;
of girls he'd had and girls he wished he'd had;
of skinny-dipping at the sandpit.

He spoke of his girlfriend and young daughter
who might come home to him *someday;*
of his dogs and cats
with names such as King, Duke, Princess and Duchess —
his houseful of royalty.

All night he talked as I listened,
wishing I could undo the hurt he had known,
hating how life chewed him up.

Once When I was Samson

Tom, the youngest pressman, walked into the breakroom where I was proofreading *Chiron Review* and having a Diet Pepsi. He had never spoken to me in all the time he'd worked at the print shop. He put his money into the candy machine, pushed a button and nothing happened.

His handsome, shy, young face looked perplexed and disappointed, though my eyes may have been primarily on his cute butt.

Having worked at the print shop long enough to know the vending machines in the breakroom were more or less a gamble, he grabbed the machine to shake it, but his hands slipped off.

I looked up from the galleys of *Chiron #32* and asked, *Machine giving you grief?*

He sighed, *Yeah, my hands are too greasy. I can't grip it to shake it loose.* I volunteered, *You want me to try?*

He said, *Yeah!*

So I stood up, faced the machine, grasped firmly and shook. Let me tell you I rocked that machine! I was Samson as he brought the temple down around his ankles. And Tom's heart's desire fell into the tray ... *PLOP!* ... a little bag of peanut M & Ms.

He smiled and said, *Thanks!* and took his M & Ms.

My smile flowed all over him, told him I was more pleased than he, told him of course I'd move heaven and earth anytime to please him; he doesn't even need to ask.

The Perfect Tape

When I was in high school,
I tried to make a cassette tape
of piano music for Aunt Sue.

Our house was tiny, crowded and noisy.

I was cranky and irritable
because no one would quit talking and laughing
long enough for me to get
the perfect tape.

I eventually gave up.

Twenty-five years later, after mother's death,
I ran across the cassette in her jewelry box
while cleaning out my parents' house.

I put it in the cassette player and pushed play.

There it was, the purpose of the whole tape —
my clumsy but ambitious piano playing.
But the music was only a noisy obstacle,
as I strained my ears for the slightest hint
of Mother's voice,

her big laughter in the background;
the lively banter of my little brothers & sister;
Grandma Smith's chatter, her *Oops!* and lilting laughter
when she remembered I was recording;
the obnoxious howl of Mother's long-gone Siamese cat —
the sounds of bustling life in our home
so many years ago.

All that beautiful chattering and giggling,
was music to my ears and I realized
if it hadn't been for that damned piano music,
it would have been the perfect tape.

poem scribbled on burger king napkin at 6:30 a.m.

An irritating idiotic joy
wrestles me —
& wins —
in spite of bombs & church fires
& evidence everywhere
that humanity has reached
the year 2000 of the Common Era
still festering,
still thriving
on selfishness, stupidity
& hatred —

in spite of knowing
someone exists somewhere
who would kill me
for how I was born,
for who and how I have loved —
& the only reason I'm still alive
is because our paths haven't crossed
yet.

This poem means nothing
except that I have watched
another golden purple sunrise.

Poetry as Talisman

Ratboy got a new cassette
by Marilyn Manson,
a rock group whose members
each chose a super model's first name
and a famous murderer's last name —
and who claim to have sold their souls
to Satan to be popular
with teenagers.

I got the mail
and found a missive
from Wilma Elizabeth McDaniel,
the *biscuits & gravy* poet.

The battle of good over evil rages on
in an unassuming cabin on the edge
of a little town in Kansas —

Marilyn Manson rapes the air —

I read Wilma's latest letter
and poetry gems —

unscathed.

postcard from California
to my lover

i woke
& remembered
there's a great
beatific world
outside
our tight hateful cocoon

it revolves
around a big fat sun
not your dick
& is infinitely
larger & more
generously
life-giving

Proposed Legislation: Never to Forget
for Milton Meltzer (1915-2009)

I read on Facebook about some guy
who sucker punched a Nazi at a rally.
The Facebook poster, a fine poet, was distraught,
lamenting the death of free speech.
He whined, *There ought to be a law!*

I agree. In the interest of Public Health,
punching Nazis should be regulated.

It should be against the law
to face punch any Nazi
coyly hiding behind the First Amendment
more than 6,000,000 times.

6,000,001 will be considered excessive force,
punishable to the full extent of the law.

The Pure Poetry That is Ratboy

As I unloaded the car,
Ratboy was engrossed in a tv wrestling match.
I gasped, *Why don't you come here*
and help me bring in the groceries?

Never taking his eyes from the tv,
he replied,
Why don't you come here
and suck a fart out of my ass?

Revelations & Anticipation

oh sweet Jesus,
hurry!

i eagerly await
Your Second Coming

when You will swoop down
like a giant Hoover

sweeping these godawful
hysterical squawking *Christians*
out of our hair.

Road Trip: Topeka, November 29, 1997

I neglected to put film in my camera so this poem will have to do. We left for Topeka Saturday, me and my housemate Rusty and his young boyfriend. We met up with our friend Dawn, visiting her grandma in Topeka. Dawn is 22, big, beautiful, butch, blond, boisterous, happy, hyper, feisty, mischievous. On Grandma's TV a wedding photo of Dawn's aunt and her aunt's new wife, two rowdy cowgirls who found love and peace in each other's arms in Topeka, Kansas in spite of Fred Phelps. At Classics, Topeka's only gay bar, disco lights revolving, flashing, music blaring and a barful of smiling gay people, gyrating to the beat, arms flying, hips twitching. *Did you think I'd crumble / Did you think I'd lay down and die?!? Oh no not I! ... I will survive!* Dawn is delightfully tipsy. She dances and sidles suggestively up to the wallflower that is always me, leering and smiling, bumping and grinding into me. I am helpless with laughter and people are watching. There is no trace of the defeated lesbian who was ganged up on by three homophobic co-workers, accused of abusing her mentally disabled charges and fired without investigation. There is no sign of her helpless acceptance of that blatant discrimination. No evidence of the heartbreak. She twinkles and shines and sings at me, *I get knocked down / but I get up again / you're never gonna keep me down! ... I get knocked down / but I get up again / you're never gonna keep me down!* She introduces us to her best childhood friend, a cute hot young Latino boy, dressed to kill. He dances free from memories of police entrapment and harassment by Topeka cops, of the humiliation of having his name printed in the

Topeka Journal, of Fred Phelps picketing his workplace and getting him fired. There is no sign of his pain, only joyful abandon as he dances: *I get knocked down, but I get up again, you're never gonna keep me down!* I see Rusty dancing, with the courage of several Rum and Cokes. Who could guess the pain and humiliation this ever-jolly soul suffered at the hands of two violent, hate-filled gay bashers? In this place where I should be happy, hearing a song that should make me want to dance with my friends, are unannounced tears, the understanding that every gentle soul in the club is dancing as hard and as fast as they can away from relentless hatred and abuse.

St. John Pastoral

an April night
just cooled by short rain
almost perfect stillness,
almost perfect quiet

but cars hum down Highway 281

some lady's calling in the distance:
Here Gandolph! Here kitty kitty kitty!

someone's guffawing down the block:
it's the cowboys on the corner
laughing, talking and yelling,
Bulllllshiiittttt!

and someone's in their yard swing
softly singing an old Carter Family tune,

If He calls me I will answer,
If He calls me I will answer,
If He calls me I will answer,
I'll be somewhere workin' for my Lord.

(that's me)

Second to Last Poem for Tracy

I offered life
scented as morning coffee,
alfalfa in bloom,
poetry at midnight,
roses, lilacs,
the very singing heart
of springtime.

He grunted, puked,
rolled joints in pages
bleeding holy poetry,
stole cars, guns,
craved cheap cigarettes,
stale beer,
and 3 a.m. whores in heat.

snapshot of me proofreading *Chiron* #53
(probably not very well) in my room,
surrounded by 11 cats on my bed
March 15, 1998, 3:30 a.m.

On the page
DougLisa Rice's words about Jesse Helms, P.H.,
(Practicing Heterosexual),
at war with practicing homosexuals —

Al Hirt's trumpet squealing *Poupée Brisée,*
my foot tapping out of control,
arms waving in mutant strain
of extinct 1960s dances.

Serena lies sprawled beside the pages,
grabbing at my pen.
I touch her butterball tummy
to the beat of the trumpet.
She nips my hand, stands,
commences *vicious* six-toed
backfeet dance on my hand.

Atop the stereo, Robin,
petite shy gold bespeckled cat,
focusses mellow eyes at me,
her neverending message:
lovelovelovelovelovelovelove —

tail twitches back and forth
over vanilla candle
tempting flame.

stumbling into light
for Z

A lifetime of clawing darkness,
head tilted at sun,
neverending clawing,
climbing upwards,
pawing at dead sky,
blind and confused animal
feeling sun, never seeing it.
Whoever is watching his life
will let go of him;
will let go of a lifetime
of catching him when he stumbles,
of saving him when he ventures too high,
of a brotherhood that was born
before any god splattered against the sky.
Whoever is watching his life
watches his wide blue blind eyes
as he struggles up his final dream.
As the climber peaks at the pinnacle
he teeters at the top —
whoever loves him most lets go
so he may stumble into light.

summer 1986

4 u i hushed 1000
barking madmen   borrowed small
prayers   summoned hot darkness
4 u i shyly offered the
touch of my warm hand
broke 7 kinds of loneliness
counted every twinkling thing
in the giggling night time sky

Sunday School

Kansas, early 1970s

She said, *In Heaven there'll be streets*
made of transparent gold
& a mansion for everybody.
I said, *Wow! ... but what do people do in heaven?*
She said, *You can do anything you want in heaven.*
I said, *Do you mean I could ride dinosaurs*
and sing with Mama Cass?!
and she said, *Uh ... i guess so.*

Talking to Squirrels

The kitties went out to play
and I sat outside to enjoy
what I love most about rural Kansas —
the serenity.

It was short-lived and interrupted
by an unholy caterwauling.
Charlie, my fat fluffy orange & white cat
ran past me with a baby squirrel in his mouth.

I seldom interfere with my cats' hunting.
When I was a little boy and would get upset
when Mom's Siamese killed birds and mice,
Dad taught me, *It's Nature, you shouldn't interfere.*

I chased Charlie around the front of the house,
where the baby squirrel struggled loose & ran.
He huddled at the side of the house,
four more cats surrounded him, eyes gleaming.

Defying Dad & Nature, I scolded Charlie,
shooed the other cats away,
scooped the baby up in a bucket,
and returned him to his home
in the crook of an ancient elm.

He scampered up the tree, then right back down.
He clung to the tree upside down at my eye-level,
neck stretched, he chattered furiously,
scolded me up one side & down the other.

I said, *I know, cats are fucking assholes.*

They Don't Write Love Stories Like This Anymore
(for Ezra & Doshia)

Although no one talked about it,
my mother's parents met through a lonely hearts ad
in a western magazine.
Grandma was about 20,
lived on her father's farm in northern Louisiana.
Granddad was 34, lived in southern Kansas,
but worked on his father's flatboat
up and down rivers
between Indiana and Louisiana.

They corresponded about four years,
married in Louisiana in 1926,
settled in central Kansas.

They survived the Depression and WWII.
They also survived raising a son and seven daughters,
who blessed them with 25 grandchildren.

In 1953, Granddad retired from 20 years
of working for the Santa Fe Railroad.

When he'd come home from work,
no matter how many kids & grandkids
were bustling about the busy household,
if Grandma Herself wasn't in the living room
he'd ask, *Where is everybody?!?*

Throwing Dirt: Remembering Julie

I was only three, but I remember the day we all met. It was a spring day in 1965. Mother was hanging clothes on the line at our little house on North Boston in Stafford, Kansas. The clothesline was parallel with the alley, which ran down the block between Boston and Keystone streets. We saw a lady (Barbara) with three little girls walking up the alley. Sandy, the oldest, the laid-back mellow one, was several paces behind her mother taking time to smell the roses. Barbara was carrying Debra, who was a baby. Julie, the active one, always in a hurry and looking for trouble, was way ahead of her mom trying to hurry her up. Barbara stopped to exchange pleasantries with Mom, and three lifetime friendships were born. Barbara became my mother's best friend.

Julie's family didn't stay in town very long, but Barbara's mother lived nearby, so with that connection, we managed to keep in touch. Julie's father, Harold, worked in the oil business. He only had a third grade education, but he was one of the smartest men I ever knew. He had an in-born knowledge and wisdom as well as mathematical genius and sharp memory that brought him excellent, high-paying jobs with oil companies.

The family moved a lot, sometimes four or five times in a year. They lived all over central Kansas and Alabama. They also lived briefly in Arkansas, Louisiana, Mississippi, Texas and for the last few years, the family lived in Missouri. I was always envious of them, that they got to move around, meet different people, change scenery, see different places, live in different houses. They told me I was lucky to have roots.

They lived mostly out of state and far away, but once in the early 1970s they lived in Lyons, not too far from our hometown. One summer day Mom had a spat with Dad and decided we were going to *run away from home*. She loaded my brother and I in the car and we spent the weekend with Harold and Barbara and the girls (who were four in number by then) in Lyons. We watched wrestling with Harold, who was a giant of a man. But he was so gentle with us and had the sweetest smile and sparkling blue eyes.

One morning we sat down to breakfast with Harold and Mom said, *Good luck getting him to eat. He won't eat anything,* referring to my brother Joe. She looked into the kitchen later and was astounded to find Joe wolfing down a hearty breakfast with Harold, who was grinning from ear to ear.

My favorite memory of our family visiting their family happened somewhere down in Texas. I was about 12. They lived in a giant house that looked like a hotel, with a long, wide hall down the middle, rooms down each side, and a bathroom at the end of the hall.

One night I heard the sounds of Elvis emanating from the kitchen about three o'clock in the morning. At our house, we didn't wander about at 3 a.m., so I was intrigued and got up to see what was going on. Julie had gotten up and was fixing a fried onion and ketchup sandwich, listening to Elvis on an old record player as loud as she could get him. She made me a sandwich too, and we just sat there, eating, talking and listening to Elvis until we were ready to go back to bed. I believe it was some time during this visit that we vowed to be *friends forever*.

Though Julie's family lived in Alabama through most of our growing up years, she spent a couple of summers with her grandmother in our town. During our junior high years, we were so very rebellious together. We ran the streets of our small town late at night. We didn't get into any trouble, but it wasn't for lack of trying! There was just simply none to be had and neither one of us would have known what to do with it if we *had* found it.

I was told Julie had spinal meningitis when she was a baby and had barely survived it, that she had *brain damage*. I never saw any evidence of that. She did quit school when she was 16, but it was because big mean girls in a new school and new town were beating her up and she just thought school was *dumb*. I'm inclined to agree with her on that.

She had a profound, no-nonsense common sense, an ability to cut right through crap and always had both feet firmly on the ground. She met reality head on and didn't waste time on crazy flights of fancy. She was eager to become an adult, to be independent. She worked steadily from the time she was 16, mostly as a cook, a vocation she loved and for which she had a natural affinity. Wherever she worked, she was respected and beloved by her bosses and co-workers, once she allowed them to get to know her.

Julie started smoking when she was eight. She stole cigarettes from her parents, who forbade her to smoke. They told her, *Do as we say, not as we do!* But Julie being Julie, kept stealing cigarettes until the day her father caught her. He decided to break her of the habit right then and there. He made her smoke every single cigarette in the pack. That stubborn, mule-headed girl sat in front of him, looked him straight in the eye and smoked every single cigarette. I don't know if she got sick or not. If she did, I guarantee it wasn't in front of her dad. And it never broke her of smoking.

As long as I knew her, she carried a cigarette case and a silver Butane lighter wherever she went. The smell of Butane reminds me of the best of times and the best of friends. I don't huff Butane or anything, but when someone lights up with a Butane lighter around me, I can't help but enjoy a brief, euphoric jaunt down memory lane.

In our early 20s Julie and Debra lived for a couple of months with me in my first house when I was 22, but that didn't go so well. Some folks got the idea we should get married, and she got that idea too. I didn't agree. This, among other things, caused a rift between us. The girls moved back to Alabama and hard feelings kept us apart for awhile, but not longer than three months. Living together was a rich learning experience for all three of us.

By the next year, they were inviting me to come and stay with them, so off I went. It was during this time in Alabama that I *came out* to Julie. I wanted her to know why I didn't marry her, that I didn't want her to be hurt, and that if I wasn't gay, I'd have married her when we were 14! Maybe 12! When I finally had the nerve to say the words, she shrugged, said something like, *So? You're still my best friend.* And that was the end of it, except she was a little miffed that I didn't trust her and tell her much sooner. She felt like she should have been the *first* person I told, and she was right.

Julie and Debra lived in an apartment a mile or so out of town. They both worked in a wonderful greasy spoon called Jay's Fine Foods just down the road, in Fayette. Being a vegetarian, I lived mostly on cottage fries, which Julie and Debra brought home after work.

Julie had an old, rusty, beat-up brown clunker of a car. If I'd have called it that to her face, I'd have gotten one of her *looks*, a swift hard punch in the arm, and maybe a pretty long silent treatment. It was her very first car and she was so proud of it. She firmly believed it was the greatest automobile to ever roll off the assembly lines at Detroit.

We took that old car to the cowboy bar in Tuscaloosa on weekends. Every now and then the engine burst into flames. She'd yell, *Get out and throw dirt!* And by God, that's what we did. She'd pop the hood and all the passengers bailed out of the car, threw dirt on the engine until the fire went out, and off we'd go in the car again. I shudder to think of doing anything like that now, but every single moment during that summer in Alabama was perfect.

After six weeks, I got so homesick I went back home to Kansas and resumed my life there. But Julie and Debra weren't far behind me. Mom and I were both delighted when the entire family moved back to central Kansas in 1986. The joy was short-lived because Julie and Debra's father died suddenly of a heart attack on Dec. 21, 1986. This tragedy hit the entire family harder than a ton of bricks. Julie never got over it, and I doubt if anyone else in the family has either.

Most of the family moved on to Missouri, but Julie stayed. We enjoyed the best years of our friendship during this time, 1986-1990. We'd both grown up some, gotten over past hurts and squabbles. We went everywhere together and had so much fun. We got curly perms together (it *was* the 80s!). We attended concerts by Randy Travis, Ronnie McDowell, The Mamas and the Papas. We hung out in bars and didn't drink. We spent hours riding around, sitting in diners, coffee shops, convenience stores, just talking, sometimes not talking, just being together.

Julie loved to wait until one of our mothers approached the car to get in. She'd wait until the perfect, precise moment, and then honk the horn. She had it down to a fine art. She loved to watch them jump and exclaim, *Oh, Julie Mae!* One might think she only did this as a small child or mischievous teen-ager, but one would be wrong. She was still doing that in her 30s!

Julie and I were truly *not* drinkers, though we did drink once in a blue moon. And even though I know alcohol is bad and blah blah blah, my favorite memories of Julie are when she was drunk.

The first time Julie, Debra and I went out and Julie got drunk was in Great Bend. The party's end found us at Love's Country Store on East 10th. Deb and I went into the store for cigarettes, pop and snacks. When we came out, Julie wasn't in the car and was no where to be found! Tenth Street is the busiest street in town and bar rush had hit. As we stood there wondering how we were going to explain to Barbara that we'd lost her #2 daughter, we heard faint strains of an Olivia Newton-John song wafting from behind the store.

We ventured back there. Julie was rummaging through the store's dumpster, singing, *Let's get physical, physical, let's get physical ... physical ... let me hear your body talk, your body talk ...* We both said, *What the hell are you doing?!?* She slurred, *Mom needs boxes!* She was simply doing a good deed, gathering boxes for her mom, who was planning a move soon.

Julie was mostly a shy, reserved, no-nonsense person. She never spoke to strangers, seldom spoke unless spoken to, sometimes not even then. At the same time, she had a dry, wry, quirky, mischievous, relentless, irrepressible sense of humor, that not everyone had the pleasure of experiencing. But, when she drank, there were no *strangers,* and that aforementioned sense of humor became full-blown and *out there* for *everyone* to enjoy.

The second time we went out drinking together, which was a few years later in Pratt, Deb and I knew from experience it was necessary to baby-sit Julie and watch her every move. After a mighty battle that finally convinced her she was *not* going to drive, we ended up at Love's Country Store on South Main in the middle of the night. Debra and I walked on each side of her. The double glass doors were propped open because it was a warm night. As Debra and I entered the store on either side of her, Julie collided full-tilt into the thick metal pole separating the two doors, which none of us had seen!

As she recovered from that, stumbling into the store, mumbling about how *mean* we were, she finally stood up straight, looked up and found herself staring eyeball to eyeball with an older policeman sitting in a booth. He was smiling from ear to ear at her antics. Normally,

Julie would have been frightened speechless of that close a proximity to a policeman or *any* stranger. But on this special night, she looked him in the eye, staggered towards him, leaned on his table, totally invading his *personal space* and slurred, *They won't let me drive when they're drunk!*

In April of 1989, Julie accompanied my friend Brad and me on a road trip to Springfield, Illinois. I'd been invited to present a lecture titled *The Art of Small Press Publishing* at Sangamon State University for the *Arts in Our Own Backyard* festival. The professors/poets/editors who'd invited me to speak, Glenn Sheldon and Rane Arroyo, invited my friend Brad, Julie and I to their house for a drink when we arrived in town.

They offered us each a Screwdriver, and we drank them down. Little did Julie and I know other folks use a bit more Vodka in their Screwdrivers than we did! All seemed well until it was time to leave. I stood up, stumbled slightly forward and caught myself just before I landed head-first in Brad's lap. Julie had a similar experience in her attempt to stand up.

Julie's and my eyes locked, knowing we were both in trouble. Brad stayed behind to visit with Glenn and Rane, while Julie and I attempted to navigate our way out of the apartment with dignity and down the steep brownstone steps. We held on to each other for dear life, grasped at the hand-rail and giggled like schoolgirls as we slowly, deliberately navigated each step, one at a time. The rest of the night is a pleasant blur.

Through the 1990s, Julie and various family members moved back and forth between Kansas and Missouri, mostly settling in Springfield. In 1993, Julie married a man named Doug in Kansas. The marriage was a disaster, but after she married, predictably, our friendship changed. We stayed in contact, but went about our separate lives. Julie separated from Doug and he died shortly after, in 2001.

We had a few more good times in passing, but Julie lived and seemed far away in her latter years. She had a lot of serious health problems, including diabetes. Even so, she seemed genuinely happy during the last four years of her life with her new companion, Bobby, and their 17 dogs. Bobby treated her like a queen and made her lifelong dream of visiting Graceland come true.

During our last phone conversation a couple of months before she died, we joked with each other about how she'd become the *crazy old dog lady* and I'd become the *crazy old cat lady.* We had a good chuckle out of that, and that was the last time I talked to her.

To John — Just a Cat

You were *just a cat,* as most farmers and our less-than-evolved fellow mid-westerners would say. Just a cat who was born in my bedroom closet 6/25/95. Just a cat who was orange & white, rabbit-soft. Just a funny loving clown-face boy. Just a butterball food lover. Just a cat we watched grow & play with three wacky siblings in a patch of weeds. As if you were tigers in the wildest of jungles. Just a friend. A dear companion. Just a lucky gift. Whose path crossed ours on this big whirligig spaceship earth. In our tiny drop of time and space.

You disappeared 2/17/99. Not knowing makes every day a heavy stone. The city burned a dilapidated house behind dad's property. Chances are you were be-bopping around there, stalking mice. Got scared of the sudden firemen and vehicles. Ran into the old house, believing you were safe. Chances are the firemen were oblivious to your sweet presence. Chances are you are dead. A victim of smoke inhalation. If I prayed, that's what I would pray. That you had a minimum of pain and fear. That I might still see you sauntering up the driveway. Your funny face and banner tail, eager for food, then love, then a warm place to take a nap. The thought of your aloneness breaks my heart. Knowing how desperate you were to run home, the place where you were loved, revered for the sacred creature you were.

It isn't natural for the snow to fall. The ice to come. The wind to blow. Knowing you're out there somewhere in it. Each day is a heavy stone. I guess we all have to meet fate. It is a terrible wait. Well, congratulations. At least you got that over with.

A Toast

Pam was the little sister of my two best childhood friends,
and our mothers were best friends.
Pam and I became close too, but she was a such a wild child,
such a gypsy gadabout,
we kept in touch but seldom saw each other.

She was a unique and fascinating character
with an irresistible charisma.
One had little choice but to love her
regardless of what she said or did.
And she did say and do some shit!

Pam was a free-thinker, as independent as they come.
She followed her impulses wherever they led her —churches,
bars, jails, marriages, the Job Corp., traveling carnivals …

She landed in Kansas for a short while after her first marriage
and a devastating miscarriage.

One fall day she picked up a young hitchhiker,
they were engaged within a few days.
Then Pam became critically ill and was admitted to a hospital.
That didn't stop the wedding.

On a September afternoon in Pratt, Kansas,
a kindly old minister from a local church
married Pam, flat on her back in a hospital bed,
to a sweet, handsome, young stranger from Alabama.

I served as best man.
A nurse wheeled in a hospital snack cart
laden with sparkling grape juice, cake, mints and nuts.
Sam would not be Pam's last husband.

A couple of decades and many adventures later,
Pam died unexpectedly in her sleep at the age of 42.
Just two weeks before, she called me. I hadn't heard from her in years.
In the middle of that four-hour chat marathon,
she suddenly ordered me not to be sad when she passed on.

Sadness is inevitable. I'll miss her,
and be sorry to know she's not out there somewhere
stirring shit up, analyzing and cackling away at the ironies,
absurdities and hypocrisies of the human condition.

But today I smile and raise a toast to my friend Pam,
enchanted soul, liberated cosmic traveler,
as she soars, laughing, to her next appointment.

Tracy Pops Into a Dream Two Years Later
Just to Let Me Know

I loved him since 7th grade — it wasn't just puppy love —
at my very first sight of him my heart skipped beats,
I was struck stupid, speechless, weak in the knees –
the very best feeling life ever offers —
it continued way into my 30s.

But my life was too tame for him.
he was discontented,
always a lost boy who didn't want to find his way.
We disconnected,
he, to find excitement, always looking for a higher high,
me, for self-preservation.

The morning after that dumb out-of-blue dream,
I was devastated to find his obituary on-line:
dead at 49, two years before.

I hadn't seen him in 22 years,
but fantasized about him out there somewhere,
surely chiseled and handsome as ever at forty-something,
his face wizened just enough to make him even sexier,
his steely hazel eyes softened with the wisdom
of age & experience.

Maybe he had a wife & children,
maybe even some grandkids?

But I should have known
when he dropped by one last time in that dream,
all squeaky-clean and dressed up in a suit & tie,
it was not to tell me he'd gotten his shit together;
it was not to tell me he was on his way to a good job,
or that he was on a date
still making girls & guys weak in the knees,
still making hearts skip beats with his sly but innocent grin.

He was dressed up for church, on the way to his own funeral.

violent virgin

god's colors drip
into timid boys
down long-legged
denim. There is a time
when god is
denim blue.
god's summer colors
drip down your lover's
thighs, into his
answering
machine
you can't touch any
thing that's holy
even if you
whisper
politely.
god drips luv,
he forgives people sinning   people
writing poems about his colors.
god's lucky luv drips all around us,
get on your knees,
lick it up.

Wanda

You were my rowdy junior high cohort.
I was bedazzled by your long, raven hair,
your blue ice eyes, your pretty smile,
your rowdy, fun-loving ways.

I don't remember why it was so funny
when we snuck up on each other from behind
and slammed each others' locker doors shut,
but at the time, it was the height of hilarity.

You said you couldn't go to church with me
because your father wanted you at home.

I can't describe how it felt
that junior high morning
when I got to school and learned
your family had moved away overnight,
without a trace.

I can't repeat what I screamed at God
when I learned your own father
had been raping you.

What She Never Told Anyone

When I was 23, I baby-sat a doctor's children
while he and his wife went out to dinner.
Upon their return, the doctor went straight to bed.
I barely knew her, but suddenly his wife said,
I've never told anyone this.

She told me how her step-father raped her,
how the doorway of her bedroom was darkened
by the shadow of her drunken stepfather,
her little-girl life broken by the groping passion
of a respected but perverted man.

She sobbed and told me when they're 12,
little girls should sleep with dolls, dogs and cats,
not drunk daddies.

She told me how she got sick, had a stomach ache,
was pregnant at age 12.
Her mother grudgingly called a doctor.
There were complications with the birth.
Grandma said, *Let the little bastard die!*
as a 12-year-old mom lost consciousness,
to wake on a blood-soaked mattress later.

Mama and baby took a late-night ride,
as an accusing, screaming grandma
reached into the backseat to slap and hit
that 12-year-old mom,
to scream unspeakable names in her face.
The *little bastard* did die.

That little girl searched the cemetery for years
for a tiny gravestone.
Nobody told her *little bastards* didn't get gravestones.

Her mother's hate festered.
She blamed her daughter for *it*,
because when your husband is *Man of the Year*,
he is too important for a scandal,
and besides, *it* didn't really happen,
but she hated her young daughter for *it* anyway.

That episode repeated itself three years later,
except a 15-year-old mom refused to return home.

A 23-year-old woman forgave her mom and stepfather.

A 44-year-old woman tells me she loves her mother,
she tells me she still loves God.

what would Grandma think?

every Saturday,
Ratboy and i jump into the car,
with a case of Keystone Light
and a bottle of Southern Comfort
and hit the highway
with no particular destination.

we find a town we think might be groovy,
rent a motel room and commence to enjoy
the finer things in life:

Diet Coke mixed lightly with
Southern Comfort,
beer chasers, delivered pizza,
Beavis & Butt-head on MTV,

wrestling and fighting during commercials,
slamming each others' heads against the walls,
power pillow fights, broken lamps,
busted ribs, jammed fingers, fistfuls of hair,
teeth marks from head to toe,
beer fights that saturate our clothes,
back flips from one bed to another ...

3 a.m. finds us exhausted, lying there,
our brains floating pleasantly
in pools of alcohol.

my eyes scope the room:
i spy the nightstand covered with beer cans,
and bottles of booze.

Grandma's sweet face flashes before my eyes,
and her stern words:
Never set anything on top of a Bible.

i respectfully, carefully
remove all the beer cans
and the Southern Comfort
off the Gideon Bible,
pretty sure Grandma is smiling
down from Heaven in approval.

When *The Hunk Flunked Bar Exams Second Time*

I said, *I'll bet John Kennedy Jr.*
will be a great president some day ...
But what if he's the third
in the 'triumvirate'
to be assassinated
as Nostradamus predicted?

Mom said, *That'll just*
go to show Ted Kennedy
wasn't worth shootin'.

Why I Love to Say Her Name Out Loud
for Suzanne

Because it is a poem in itself.
She is a poem likewise,
without realizing it —
the way she distributes joy
to each life she touches
without losing anything,
the way she allows things to be funny
laughing honestly,
how she hugs God,
how He lives through her.

Winter Snapshot 2011

In my tiny cozy living room,
I'm surrounded by cats of many colors,
shapes and sizes—
they #OccupyTheLivingRoom in protest
of snow and winter chill.
They wash up and settle in for the night.

Roxanne, multicolored Maine Coon,
decrees Herself infinitely more important
than any MacBook,
sprawls the Entire Regal Self
across my forearms as I type.

Responsibility for all typos
may be laid at The Royal Feet.

Michael Hathaway lives in St. John, Kansas in his childhood home with his family of felines. By day, he works as Keeper of History for Stafford County, and by night edits and publishes *Chiron Review* literary journal which he founded in 1982. He's worked many day jobs to enable his poetry habit including newspaper typesetter/compositor, society editor, librarian, janitor, chauffeur, painter, wallpaperer, ladies clothing store clerk, babysitter, pet-sitter, house-sitter, and living assistant to the mentally disabled. He served 12 years on the Goodman Library city board, and currently serves as secretary/treasurer for the Stafford County Central Democratic Party. In 2008, he accidentally became an ordained minister of Spiritual Science (which has its roots in Theosophy and Gnosticism). He's had 12 books of poetry and prose published, as well as 300+ poems in journals and anthologies. He was founding chairman of Poetry Rendezvous that celebrated its 30th anniversary in 2018. For more information about *Chiron Review*: http://www.chironreview.com.

www.ingramcontent.com/pod-product-compliance
Lightning Source LLC
Chambersburg PA
CBHW020123130526
44591CB00032B/393